A full year
Bulletp

52 Bulletproof Leadership Tips

Volume 2

A Continuing Series to Help Improve Employee Morale, Accountability, and Performance

Chief Ronald C. Glidden (Ret.)

Ronald C. Glidden

Copyright © 2016 Ronald C. Glidden
Editing: Carole Glidden
Cover image: 123RF®

All rights reserved. No part of this book may be reproduced or transmitted in any form or by any means without the written permission of the author. Requests for permission to photocopy any portion of this book for any use should be directed to the address below.

Printed in the United States of America.

First printing, August 2016

ISBN: 978-0-692-75418-4

Published by:
Gold Badge Publishing
PO Box 73
South Wellfleet, MA 02663
www.ronglidden.com

52 Bulletproof Leadership Tips

Volume 2

Contents

Acknowledgements and Subscription Information .. 1
Introduction 2
<u>The 52 Tips</u>
#1: Cultivating Real Top Performers 4
#2: Never Too Smart 8
#3: The 7 Step Accountability Process 12
#4: Practice 15
#5: Apologies 19
#6: Workplace Hazing, Bullying and Harassment .. 23
#7: New Appointment or Promotion 28

#8:	Self-Doubts	32
#9:	Advocates Are Not Gossips	35
#10:	Sincere and Specific Appreciation	38
#11:	Effective Meetings	42
#12:	Career Mentors	45
#13:	Managing B Players	49
#14:	Supervisors Appreciating Supervisors	53
#15:	Unappreciated Appreciation	57
#16:	Working With Extroverts	61
#17:	Saboteurs	65
#18:	Telephone Basics	68
#19:	Think They Know It All People	71
#20:	Imposter Syndrome	74
#21:	Overly Sensitive Employees	77
#22:	Ownership Psychology	81
#23:	The Disgruntled Employee	84
#24:	Cultivating Ideas	87
#25:	Limitations of the Written Word	90
#26:	Not Funny	93
#27:	Hobby Time	97
#28:	Sarcasm	100
#29:	Chronic Complainers	103
#30:	Real Engagement	106

#31:	Predictability	109
#32:	Rule Benders	112
#33:	Attention to Details	115
#34:	Space Cadets	118
#35:	Sincerity	121
#36:	Fault Finders	124
#37:	The Blame Game	127
#38:	What We Control	130
#39:	Coaching	134
#40:	Sick Leave Abuse	137
#41:	No Surprises Please	141
#42:	Unacceptable Behavior Categories	144
#43:	Recognition – It's in the Details	147
#44:	Getting Along	150
#45:	The Purpose of Training	153
#46:	The Supervisor as Protector	156
#47:	Improvement Is Not Enough	159
#48:	Messy Bessy	163
#49:	Specialty Entitlement	167
#50:	When to Speak Up	171
#51:	When There Is No Answer	174
#52:	When Accountability Is a New Concept	178
	Speaker Information and Book Orders	182

Ronald C. Glidden

Acknowledgments

Thank you to our nation's public safety professionals who put their lives on the line to help keep our families safe. Thank you also to my seminar attendees and weekly *Bulletproof Leadership Tip* subscribers. Your support, frequent questions and continual feedback have made this second volume of leadership tips possible.

Sign up to receive your FREE weekly *Bulletproof Leadership Tips*

If you are not already a subscriber, sign up today to receive your FREE weekly *Bulletproof Leadership Tips* by email. To subscribe, go to www.RonGlidden.com and click on the "Sign Me Up" button.

Ronald C. Glidden

Introduction

When I wrote the first 52 leadership tips that made up what was to become the first volume of *52 Bulletproof Leadership Tips*, I based much of that work on the bosses, coworkers, and subordinates with whom I had worked over many years. In my leadership efforts, I know I made many mistakes; but, hopefully, along the way, I got a few things right. I understood then, as I do now, the importance of the concept "Never stop learning."

Throughout my career, I attended leadership seminars and conferences, read leadership books, and listened to leadership CDs (and audio cassettes before that). I would take in all the information on leadership I could find, filter it through my own experiences or current situations, and try to apply what I thought made sense to me at that time.

Sometimes my efforts worked, and sometimes they failed miserably. Sometimes they appeared to be working only to have a "people problem" arise seemingly out of nowhere and almost derail months of what I thought were my best trust-building efforts. What I came to realize is that there is no magic potion or quick fix that works for every leader all the time. There is no remedy that works perfectly for every problem employee. There is only your best effort and continual development as you try to do what is right.

I ran into a former coworker once at a conference. It had been many years since he had worked for me. He had been a motivated, hardworking employee, and it did not surprise me that he had become a supervisor. After the conference, he came up to me and said with a smile (in his normal attempt at sarcastic humor), "How come you didn't always do everything you talked about today?" My attempt at a good natured response was, "I didn't know what I didn't know back then, but I'm much smarter now." I was trying to be funny, but there was truth in my response. The fact is that we should all be working to be better leaders tomorrow than we were yesterday.

It was with the thought of helping leaders be better at their job tomorrow than they were yesterday that I first began writing my weekly *Bulletproof Leadership Tips*. The first 52 of those tips were compiled into my first leadership book, *52 Bulletproof Leadership Tips*. The response to that initial work was so great that it inspired me to continue to provide the tips on a weekly basis and to compile this volume, also consisting of *52 Tips*. It is my sincere hope that these tips will help you improve the commitment of your employees to you and your organization. Improve **commitment** and you will improve **results**!

Tip #1

Cultivating Real Top Performers

For many years, leadership trainers have espoused the theory that the typical workforce is split into three performance tiers. This includes: 10% at the top, who are self-motived high achievers; 10% at the bottom, who think they are doing you a favor just for showing up for work; and 80% in the middle, who are your average employees. Unfortunately, we spend 80% of our time with that 10% at the bottom.

We know that some employees do not meet our minimum standards, and should be held accountable. We know we should weed out their unacceptable behavior. And if that does not work, weed out the person. But this tip is not about those problem employees at the bottom. Let's look at the top performers. Who are they, how did they get there, and are they really always top performers?

There is always the possibility that you inspired a below-average worker to suddenly change into a top performer. More likely, however, your top performer has always been a top performer even before he worked for you. You describe him with simple phrases in his annual performance review: "Strong work ethic; Self-motivated;

Needs little or no supervision." He is task-focused, and clearly seems to enjoy the job – when he gets to do the parts of the job he likes. If productivity alone were the only concern, this guy would be your hero. In fact, quite honestly, his statistics probably make you look good. They certainly do not hurt as a counterbalance to the statistics generated by the bottom 10% of your workforce.

But to get into the high achievers club – that top 10-20% of the work force - it takes, or should take, more than just generating statistics. Obviously, you have to have integrity and honesty, as well as initiative and self-motivation. You clearly have to have a good work ethic. But maybe less obvious is that you should also have respect for your coworkers and the people you serve.

Too many of today's high achievers view these characteristics as unneeded soft skills. They get along with you, of course, because you are the boss. But many of them see no need to communicate with coworkers any more than absolutely required. They do not participate in your Christmas and retirement parties. They are visibly angry at coworkers for being lazy. They are sometimes angry at you for not doing enough to hold the underachievers accountable. They sometimes even generate more civil complaints (which means work for you) than the employees in the bottom 10% of the workforce.

It is a hard problem to fix. Why? Because we like those numbers, so we sometimes give them a pass on the occasional citizen complaint. We also know that these high achievers are not usually good at accepting negative feedback. Sometimes they respond with a negative attitude, and might even sound a little angry and disrespectful that you would question their hard work. Sometimes they threaten to become just like "those other guys" (implying the bottom 10%).

Here are some suggestions for dealing with self-motivated, hardworking people, who also happen to lack essential people skills, and whose productivity you are not convinced is worth the headaches they cause.

- **Identify a behavior as a behavior.** Treating coworkers or the public with disrespect is not an attitude. It is a behavior, and this behavior is unacceptable.

- **Counsel the employee.** Let them know that top performance includes respect for coworkers and the public and is more important than statistics. Top statistics and top performance is not the same. One is about numbers and one is about results. Strive for top performance.

- **Be specific when pointing out the behaviors you find unacceptable.** Telling the employee he just needs to be "nicer" or "more professional" is not likely to get you the results you want. Generic statements are too subjective and leave too much room for interpretation.

- **Document counseling sessions.** Document what he was counseled for, and document that the employee acknowledged that he understood your expectations and will make an effort to change.

- **Know what you can and cannot change.** You cannot change attitudes, make employees like everyone, or force them to go to off-duty functions. But you can require an employee to act respectfully towards coworkers, supervisors, and the public.

- **Soft Skills are not an option.** Employees must understand that getting along with coworkers and being generally professional at work is not an option. It is an essential part of the job for which he was hired. In fact, he would not have been hired if anyone thought he was not fully capable of utilizing those skills.

TIP: Cultivate top performers who understand their job is to help the organization accomplish its overall mission and not simply generate numbers (even though you might appreciate those numbers). This requires them to get along with people including their coworkers.

Tip #2

Never Too Smart

At a recent training I conducted for supervisors, the hosting organization distributed evaluations. I had the opportunity to take a quick look before I left the classroom. There were some real ego boosters in the pile. One said, "Best leadership training I've attended to date." Another typical one said, "Should be required for all supervisors." Another one said, "Polished speaker did a great job." As I was patting myself on the back for these evaluations, I came to the last one. The unnamed attendee had written in some detail that he thought the leadership information was more appropriate for first-line supervisors than people like himself (I have no idea what rank he held).

I got the general sense from his comment that he thought upper management should be trained only in some newer, special leadership concepts (maybe some super-secret stuff). What bothered me the most was that he thought that good leadership fundamentals, concepts, and strategies only apply to lower-level or first-line supervisors and that some other type of leadership must apply to people in upper management.

What this particular supervisor could not have known is that having traveled the country talking to supervisors from over 1000 organizations, I've learned one interesting fact. Morale killers are not always our subordinates. Talk to a room full of front-line supervisors anywhere in the country and ask them to identify their biggest morale killer. About 50% of the time they will tell you it is one of their supervisors. I've had seminar attendees (supervisors of various ranks) tell me about high-ranking and highly educated bosses who were seemingly clueless with regards to the damage they do to morale, trust, and performance in their organization.

In one class, I asked attendees to write down the name of their #1 morale killer. Seven middle management supervisors from the same organization showed me they had all written down the same name – a supervisor one step above them. That morale killing supervisor was not in the class. Looking back on that now, I wonder if that particular morale killing supervisor thought he was of too high a rank to pay attention to basic leadership strategies or was too smart to attend the class.

Here are a few thoughts on the basics with regard to rank and position:

- **Good leadership is good leadership regardless of rank.** The basics of building trust, communicating clearly, holding people accountable, and showing appreciation for good work applies to all ranks. It is inconceivable to me that someone would think they have moved past these essentials by virtue of rank or promotion.

- **We are never too smart.** It would be great if our promotion came with a big dose of new smarts, more common sense, and enhanced leadership knowledge. Unfortunately, we get what we earn - when it comes to smarts - either by formal learning or by experience. We have to work at it continuously. We need the occasional formal training and the occasional refresher (we tend to forget the basics when we get busy). Sometimes we need the same info explained a different way (a different book or different training on the same topic).

- **It is not secret stuff.** Sound leadership principles are not secrets. I once had a supervisor who attended my training ask me if I was really going to teach the same things to his subordinate supervisors who were attending the class the following day. He said, "They'll know what we are doing." It is OK if they know you are working on getting better at doing what you are supposed to do.

- **It is not new.** There are few, if any, NEW leadership ideas, just new ways of explaining concepts. I first learned about "Management by walking around" from Jack Enter at an IACP conference in the 1990s. In 2000, I read about a similar concept in Stephen Covey's *The 7 Habits of Highly Effective Leadership*. It is a concept that came out of a 1982 book by Tom Peters and Robert Waterman called *In Search of Excellence*. In 2003, Quint Studer put a new spin on the same concept for the healthcare industry in his book, *Hardwiring Excellence*. Colin Powell talks about the importance of the same concept to the success of his career in his 2012 book, *It Worked For Me*. According to Donald Phillips in his book, *Lincoln on Leadership*, even Abraham Lincoln practiced the concept.

When it comes to good leadership, there are literally dozens of ways to say or learn the same concept. And I suggest you look at all of them, and then look at them again. We are never too smart to learn something new, or hear it in a different way that might stick with me better than the last time I heard it. Clearly, we are never too smart to be reminded occasionally of what is right. And we are certainly never too high up in rank to continue learning, or trying to improve.

TIP: The best leaders, regardless of rank or position, are lifelong students of leadership. They never stop reading, listening, learning, and applying what they have learned.

Tip #3

The 7 Step Accountability Process

What is the one employee behavior that bothers you the most? Sometimes a behavior bothers us, but we ignore it in hopes of avoiding conflict. Sometimes we feel the behavior has become so common (albeit unacceptable) that it has become part of the organizational culture, making it appear normal. And sometimes we do not address the behavior because we are just not sure how to handle the situation.

Supervisors across the country share similar problem employee stories. Fortunately, there are common solutions to many employee problems. In my research on this subject, I came to realize that a time-saving process for addressing unacceptable behavior might be developed that would cover most problem behaviors. The Merriam-Webster Dictionary defines a *process* as "a series of actions that produce something or that lead to a particular result." That is what I needed – a series of actions that would lead to a particular result. More importantly, I wanted my process to be repeatable. I wanted to be able to use the same problem-solving process on most, if not all, examples of unacceptable employee behavior. The good news is that a successful process is repeatable. The even better news is that a process can be learned by anyone. Here are the seven steps that are part of my process for dealing with unacceptable employee behavior.

1. **Identify the Specific Problem Behavior.** Determine that the behavior that you want to change is an actual behavior (an observable act) and not a non-specific attitude or feeling. You cannot order feelings to be changed.

2. **Determine the Performance Gap.** Identify your performance expectations and the employee's actual performance. Know how much of a gap exists and what needs to be done to close the gap.

3. **Determine Impact.** What are the consequences to the organization, the mission, or to coworkers if the unacceptable behavior continues?

4. **Determine Consequences.** What are the consequences the employee will face if he does not change his behavior to meet your expectations? Consequences may include additional supervision, loss of choice assignments, poor performance evaluations, or progressive discipline.

5. **Create A Plan.** Plan a strategy for the specific circumstances (the particular inappropriate

behavior) and the individual employee that will help you achieve the results you want.

6. **Have a Performance Discussion.** Give specific feedback to the employee to let him know exactly what behavior you determined is inappropriate, why it is inappropriate, and what he needs to change to meet your expectations. If it is a repeated inappropriate behavior, advise the employee of potential consequences for not changing.

7. **Follow Up.** If the behavior changes, acknowledge it by showing appreciation. If the inappropriate behavior does not change, provide additional counseling and/or disciplinary consequences.

TIP: Get in the habit of using a repeatable process for dealing with unacceptable employee behaviors, a process which will allow you to specifically identify the problem, create a solution, and let you know when you have succeeded. Remember, it is always about results.

Tip #4

Practice

Several years ago while on vacation in Nashville Tennessee, my wife and I decided to take a backstage tour of the Grand Ole Opry. The tour included a photo opportunity for anyone who wanted to stand in the center of the stage while holding a guitar. My wife took them up on the offer. When it was over, she told me she had always wanted to learn to play the guitar, but that she was now too old. I encouraged her to take lessons. "You're never too old to learn something new," I said. "Why don't you join me?" she replied. "I'm too old," I said. "More importantly, I have no interest in learning the guitar."

Later that night we were back at the Grand Ole Opry for a show. The last performer of the evening was Charlie Daniels. Charlie played a couple songs on his guitar, and then pulled out his fiddle and played his Grammy winning hit "The Devil Went Down to Georgia." The crowd loved it and gave him a standing ovation. When the show was over and we were walking back to the car, I confessed that I had thought about learning the fiddle when I first heard "Devil Went Down to Georgia" on the radio in 1979." On our way back to the hotel we encouraged each other to pursue our individual musical interests.

A week later I was searching the internet for a fiddle instructor. I came across a website for Megan Lynch Chowning. Megan is a six-time national fiddle champion, and has performed with country music stars like Pam Tillis and Lorie Morgan. Megan lives outside of Nashville, but offers lessons online via Skype. What really got my attention was the section of her website that said, "You can be a *Fiddle Star* whether you start playing at three or 73." Now there's a criteria I could meet. When I talked to Megan, she said, "Yes, I can teach you, but there are three things you must agree to before we start." Here is a summary of her requirements:

1. You must be willing to engage in *deliberate practice.* Deliberate practice means you structure your practice so you get something out of it every time, whether the practice is for 10 minutes or an hour. Deliberate practice is not sitting on the couch watching television while you try to play a few notes. It is not the length of the practice that is important, but the quality of the effort.

2. You must be willing to engage in practice that is repeatable. You have to be able to practice something numerous times to achieve the proficiency you desire. At least part of your practice needs to be structured so you can repeat it

regularly in order for you to be able to determine where you are improving and where you need to focus more effort.

3. You must be willing to expand your comfort zone. The majority of new adult music students quit after a few months because they become stagnant in acquiring new skills. They play the same thing over and over because they have become comfortable with something they have learned and are no longer willing to experience the discomfort of learning something new.

While traveling home from a police chief's conference recently, I was reflecting on how Megan's advice on achieving musical goals might help me in achieving leadership goals. Here is my take on how something as seemingly unrelated as the process for learning a musical instrument can help with improving your leadership ability.

- **Deliberate Practice.** Reading about leadership is not practice. Taking what you read and trying to implement what you have learned can be practice. Do you want to build trust? Put a practice plan together and implement that plan. Spend a little time each day working on it to develop your skills. You will not develop better leadership skills by accident. Real improvement requires deliberate practice.

- **Regularly Repeated.** Do not try to implement a leadership strategy just once and decide it failed or succeeded on that one effort. Real improvement requires your *deliberate practice* to be regularly repeated. That is why planning your strategy is so important. If you do not know what your personal leadership improvement plan is, you will never be able to repeat it or improve on it.

- **Expand Your Comfort Zone.** If your comfort zone is working on tasks, but you are not good at people skills, you know where you need to concentrate your efforts. Most of us have some aspect of leadership we feel comfortable with, while we lack skills or feel uncomfortable in other areas. To be successful, we have to be good at a lot of leadership skills, even some we do not particularly enjoy. Make sure at least some of your *deliberate practice,* which is *regularly repeated,* actually expands your *comfort zone.*

TIP: By its very nature, practice encourages us to stretch past our comfort zone, make mistakes, and learn from those mistakes. When it comes to applying leadership strategies, practice might not make perfect, but it does make for improvement.

Tip #5

Apologies

Have you ever made a mistake at work where you felt required to apologize to a subordinate? Good leadership requires us to continue to grow, try new things, and move past our comfort zones to improve performance. In doing so, we are bound to make mistakes. I have had countless supervisors give me examples describing situations in which they felt they were mistreated by their bosses and, subsequently, felt a loss of trust towards that boss. Consider these examples:

- An employee comes back to work after bereavement leave. His immediate supervisor asks where he has been for the past few days. The employee mentions his father had died. The supervisor changes the subject and begins talking about himself without offering any condolences.

- An employee is out of work for months due to a serious illness. No one from his organization ever came to the hospital or called during those months to see if the employee was even alive.

- An employee appears sad to his coworkers and relates that his 14-year-old Labrador Retriever died that morning. His supervisor makes a joke about it being "just a dog."

- An employee asks for a day off. His supervisor says he is too busy to approve now, but tells him to come back tomorrow. The next day the employee learns that his supervisor took the rest of the week off and no one else can approve the requested day off.

These may seem like minor incidents, but if you have experienced similar circumstances you know you felt a loss of trust in the offending supervisor. As a result, your attitude and performance sometimes suffered. Busy supervisors occasionally fail to realize that some of the things they say, do, or even joke about can have a serious impact on employee morale.

Is there a fix for such a loss of trust? Actually there is. It is called a sincere apology. If you determine you did something, or failed to do something, that caused a loss of trust, a sincere apology might minimize some of the damage and may even build a little trust. Like all humans, you make mistakes, but as a good supervisor you can recover. Acknowledge the mistake, take responsibility, and try your best not to repeat the mistake.

A police chief once asked me, "Shouldn't our employees give us a pass on some of these mistakes?" He said he had known his subordinates for many years. He was one of them before he was promoted. He thought they should know he would never do anything to hurt them. Because of that long relationship, he thought they should trust him and automatically forgive him when he screwed up or said something inappropriate out of anger. I advised him not to count on getting a "pass" either from a new or veteran employee or even from so-called work friends. If it happens, great. But do not hold your breath waiting for automatic forgiveness without giving a sincere apology.

Here are a few guidelines for apologizing when you realize you have made a withdrawal from the trust account:

- Evaluate what went wrong, what you said or should have said, or what you did or should have done. Evaluate the damage and who was impacted. Do this quickly, because while you are figuring it out, those affected are getting angry.

- The teachable moment is yours, not theirs. Do not preach to subordinates about what they should learn from your mistake.

- No Excuses. If you want to give a sincere apology, then apologize. Say you are sorry. Do not give excuses to try to mitigate your screw up.

- Private apologies are appropriate in many circumstances, especially when it is a private matter that involves a single individual.

- Public apologies are appropriate if your actions or inactions affected a larger group.

- Do not apologize for things that do not deserve your apology. There are plenty of actions we must take as supervisors for which our employees will not be happy. Do not water down your role as a supervisor by apologizing for everything.

TIP: If you think you have made a withdrawal from your trust account, a sincere apology can minimize the damage and might even put a little trust back in your account.

Tip #6

Workplace Hazing, Bullying and Harassment

I probably watch too many reality television shows for my own good. But my reason for watching them is that I like to watch the personal interaction between people and how they deal with personality conflicts and workplace issues. One show I enjoy watching is the *Deadliest Catch*. On one episode, the fishing vessel Wizard highlighted the trials and tribulations of a greenhorn (a new employee).

The greenhorn was ordered to participate in what was said to be one of the boat's traditions. Crew members were expected to have their heads shaved and received a so-called Mohawk haircut. The greenhorn refused to participate. Interestingly, there appeared to be other crew members who also did not participate. Nonetheless, the senior deckhand took great offense to the greenhorn for choosing not to get his haircut. He said the haircuts were a tradition and brought them good luck in their efforts to catch crab.

With reality television, it is sometimes hard to tell what is real and what was edited to put a particular slant on an episode. But one thing seems clear about this particular episode. The senior deckhand was extremely angry at the greenhorn for not getting his haircut. Throughout the episode, this senior employee continued to belittle, demean, and, in some cases, threaten the greenhorn. It appeared to go far beyond typical banter for the sake of humor or teamwork. At one point, the senior crewmen threw something at the greenhorn, striking him in the chest.

As the violence, or threat of violence, appeared to escalate, so, too, did the greenhorn's frustration. As the newest employee, he could say or do little to stop the harassment. All the time this was going on, the boat's captain - from his vantage point in the wheelhouse - was able to hear and see the increasing tension between the crewmembers.

Finally the greenhorn decided that the only way to put a stop to the harassment (apparently he felt he couldn't go to the captain since the captain did not seem to care) was to physically assault the senior crewmember. Only at that point did the captain intervene, scream, yell, threaten, and assault the greenhorn for assaulting the senior crewmember. It was clear the captain's loyalties were with the longstanding and very hardworking senior employee. Understandable to a degree, but his blatant taking of sides in this case seemed inappropriate.

As interesting as these interactions were to watch, the online comments on various computer forums following the show were even more interesting. Many people commented about what they thought was clearly workplace bullying or hazing. But a large number of individuals commented that they thought there was no bullying or hazing and that the greenhorn should have just gone along with the haircut as a sign that he was a team player. One person posted a comment that said, "He wasn't bullied, he was just asked to cut his hair as part of a tradition to fit in with the guys. He refused. He deserved all the grief he got after that."

Herein lies the problem. There are differing views of what is acceptable to build camaraderie and what is hazing. There are different views on banter versus harassment. Most states have a legal standard on hazing, bullying, and harassment. There may even be different standards for criminal versus civil penalties.

A supervisor should not assume that simply because the circumstance does not rise to a crime, that the behavior should be considered appropriate. Too often we hear senior employees (and sometime supervisors) talking about an employee's reluctance to participate in a tradition or go along with a practical joke as that employee not having a thick enough skin or not wanting to be part of the team. Good-natured banter and humor can build teamwork and camaraderie. However, behavior that embarrasses or demeans a person in the name of fitting in with the crew creates a hostile work environment and an angry employee.

Supervisors should be fully aware of the definitions for hazing, bullying, and harassment that apply in their jurisdiction. In some cases, failure to report or investigate certain types of behaviors can be a crime itself. And if it does not rise to the level of a crime, many times such unacceptable behaviors will rise to the level of a lawsuit. If you are fortunate enough that the unacceptable behavior does not meet the criteria for either a crime or a civil suit, know that failure to act can certainly result in a loss of trust and ongoing conflict between coworkers.

If you want to build trust with all of your employees and show them that you care for their well-being, you need to be there for all of your employees , not just the most senior ones. Do not pick sides just because one employee already participated in or may have originated a longstanding tradition. Here are some ways in which you can help build trust with all employees on this issue:

- Make sure any banter or good-natured humor you observe does not evolve into harassing, demeaning, or discriminatory behavior.

- Pay attention to longstanding traditions to make sure they do not rise to the level of hazing. Hazing is typically associated with educational settings, but is also unacceptable in the workplace.

- Investigate all complaints of workplace harassment, bullying, or discrimination.

- Even well intentioned banter can have negative psychological consequences on some employees. If it appears that an employee is bothered by what most others consider routine and acceptable humor, meet with the employee in private to determine how he views the so-called humor. Remember some employees may already be suffering from depression or other personal issues, and the banter, humor, or practical jokes could make matters worse.

- Do not wait for unacceptable behavior to reach the level of being a crime or a potential lawsuit before taking action

TIP: If we want employees to treat the public well, we should make sure they are treated well in the workplace, not only by supervisors, but by their coworkers. What is funny for one employee might not be funny to another, but what's right is always right.

Tip #7

New Appointment or Promotion

Sometimes when we are appointed to a new position we inherit a mess. Sometimes we create the mess. It would be easy if we could just blame our predecessor for past mistakes and then come up with a miracle cure to fix all the organization's problems. Too bad it is not that easy.

If you are in charge today, do not continue to blame someone who is no longer in the position. There is a ton of advice available for new supervisors - everything from do not make changes right away, to be decisive and make lots of changes immediately. Sometimes it is hard to know which piece of advice to take. The reality is that whatever you do will depend on your position, the organization, the individuals you supervise, their personalities, and your ability to work within that complex framework. It is hard for a new supervisor to be both consistent and flexible, but that is what is required.

Different circumstances will require different actions, but your character and level of professionalism should be unflinching. That professionalism must extend to your public comments regarding your predecessor. If you did not know your predecessor, assume that he was different from you, may have had a different leadership style, but probably did a good job. If it is clear that he did not do a good job, keep those thoughts and comments to yourself, move ahead, and make necessary changes. After all, you are in charge now.

Maybe you have come to realize that your predecessor simply wasn't up to the challenge of the position. Maybe he was forced out of the position. If so, make changes because those changes will benefit the organization and not just because they are different from the way your predecessor did the job.

If there are valuable processes in place created by your predecessor, do not throw out the baby with the bathwater. It makes no sense to make changes just because you want to disassociate yourself with the past. If the past contains material or processes that were useful, then use them. If such processes are outdated or inefficient, then make the change because the change is good for the organization and not because it is different from the way it was done before.

Here are a few basics guidelines for anyone being appointed or promoted to a new position.

- **Over-communicate.** A new leader can create excitement, anticipation, and nervousness in the workforce. Be as open and transparent about what you are thinking as quickly as possible. If you are generally reserved, come out of your comfort zone, so your subordinates can get to know you. You may not know what you plan to do yet, but you can talk about your values, priorities, and observations.

- **Ask a lot of questions.** Do not assume you know it all. Questions make subordinates feel you are interested in what they do and how they do it.

- **Be consistently enthusiastic and positive.** Even if you feel uncertainty and dread about the organization or your abilities, be positive and lead by example.

- **Lead by doing.** Do not be afraid to get your hands dirty. It is good to show subordinates you can do the job or - if you do not know their job - that you are, at least, not afraid of learning their job.

- **Watch for special interests.** New supervisors are usually bombarded by special interest employees. Some have a grudge, and some just have crazy ideas. Listen to everyone, but act only when you determine it is appropriate.

- **Do not change for the sake of changing.** Change is normally good. It is how we progress. But change is also uncomfortable and should not be undertaken lightly. Change because it is good for the organization and not just because it is a different way of doing something than your predecessor.

- **Do not throw out good ideas.** Just because you did not invent it or think of it first does not mean it is not a good idea. Sometimes that horrible predecessor's idea might be a better way to do it than yours.

TIP: New supervisors must take responsibility for those they supervise. You cannot continually blame people who were previously in your current position for your current troubles. We do not have to like our predecessor (and sometimes we do not), but we should use what he left that was good and improve on what he left that was bad, without any personal animosity.

Tip #8

Self-Doubts

Do you ever have moments when you think back to a simpler time in your career when you had less responsibility? Do you ever ask yourself, "What the heck was I thinking when I took this job?" Maybe things are not going as well as you expected. Maybe you think your boss saw some talent in you that you are not sure really exists. Now you are terrified he might find out you really do not know absolutely everything you should. Your boss or your subordinates might discover the truth - you are just human.

If you occasionally have self-doubts about your leadership abilities, you are certainly not alone. Every supervisor you will ever meet - if he is being honest - will tell you that they have had occasional doubts about their abilities. Having doubts about our abilities is natural. Two of our nation's greatest leaders, George Washington and Abraham Lincoln, had doubts - lots of them. Why should you be any different?

We try to put on a good show. We try to do the right thing. Most people succeed doing the right thing most of the time, but there is always that nagging question of whether we should have done something differently - or better. As managers and supervisors, we sometimes get so little feedback ourselves that it is hard to know if we are any good at our jobs. Mere survival is not an indicator. Plenty of bad supervisors survive year after year with their subordinates counting the days until their boss retires. Measuring ourselves against our peers, our boss, the guy that had the job before us, or someone doing the same job in another organization, are also poor indicators of our own abilities. So it is easy to see why we have these occasional doubts.

On those days when you are thinking you should have stayed in your previous position, keep these factors in mind:

- **Everyone has doubts.** Every person in a leadership role occasionally has self-doubts. Understand they are a normal part of leadership, but do not let them overwhelm you or negatively influence your attitude or behavior.

- **Do not be afraid of smart people.** If you can, surround yourself with people smarter than you. Utilize their knowledge for the benefit of the organization, and give them credit when deserved.

- **Subordinates may be more skilled.** There may be subordinates who are better at their job than you were when you were in their position. You did not get promoted to become a high-paid copy of your subordinates. Let them be experts at their tasks. Your job is to help them perform even better.

- **You will never have all the answers.** You do not need all the answers, but you, at least, need to know where they can be found. No one likes a know-it-all anyway.

- **Different skill sets.** If you were promoted because you were the best at your old job, understand that what got you here will not keep you here. New job skills must be developed over time.

- **Do not share your self-doubts with subordinates.** Share your doubts with a trusted friend, mentor, or your significant other, but not your subordinates. They should view you as competent and confident, with a high dose of integrity and humanity, and as someone who occasionally makes mistakes. You do not need to tell them that you do not think you should have been promoted. If that is true, they will figure it out on their own.

TIP: It is OK to have occasional self-doubts about your leadership ability as long as you do not let them poison your attitude. Use those self-doubts to motivate yourself to continue to endeavor to fill your own competency gaps.

Tip #9

Advocates Are Not Gossips

Gossip is the character assassination of, or derogatory comments towards, a fellow employee who is not present to defend himself. Policies do not stop gossip. Only supervisors who want to stop morale killing behavior and who are committed to building trust can stop gossip. Even then it can be stopped only if they observe it and take immediate action.

Most supervisors acknowledge that gossip is a problem. Most agree they should stop it when it happens in front of them. Occasionally, however, supervisors come up with a question which has caused them to hesitate on stopping this unacceptable behavior. Here are some of those questions and my responses.

Q. What if the employee has a personal problem (such as an alcohol problem) and his coworkers are talking about him because they want to help? Is that gossip?

A. Gossip is "character assassination." It is not about helping anyone. If you are having a conversation about a coworker out of spite or meanness, it is gossip. If you are having the conversation because you want to know the best way to help the coworker, that is called caring.

Q. What if two supervisors are talking about a problem employee and his unacceptable behavior? Is that gossip?

A. Your job is to help your employees perform better at their job. We do not always have all the answers. Sometimes we need advice from our supervisor peers who may have more experience. Talking to a peer or a boss about how to handle an employee problem is not gossip, it is your job.

Q. What if my subordinate talks about one of his peers. He says he is lazy and stupid, and I agree. Is that gossip?

A. The reason for stopping gossip is twofold. First, it is inappropriate and can hurt morale either because it gets back to the person involved, or it encourages more gossip from other employees. Hearing that your peers think you are lazy and stupid is not going to make you a better (or smarter) employee. Secondly, gossip damages trust. Hearing that your supervisor was in on the conversation about your laziness and stupidity is not going to make you trust your supervisor - or work harder for him. A supervisor who puts a stop to gossip (even when he might agree with what is being said) is a person employees can respect and trust.

Q. What if my subordinates are talking about another supervisor or my boss in a derogatory manner? Shouldn't I be an advocate for my employees and allow them to vent?

A. Venting which occurs in a group setting is usually unproductive, seldom leads to a resolution of the problem, and typically worsens morale. Agreeing with employee gripes about other supervisors does not build camaraderie with your employees. It damages the morale of the organization and hurts your own credibility. The cost is high and it is paid in their future lack of trust in you.

If you want to be an advocate for your subordinates, listen to their concerns, help identify the problem, help find a solution if possible, and help determine the next step to alleviate or minimize the problem. If it is just a complaint for the sake of complaining, ask for specifics if you think you can help solve a problem or put an end to it.

If it is gossip, spiteful, and mean-spirited - even if it is true - and even if you agree with what they are saying, it should not be tolerated.

TIP: Participating in or condoning gossip - even when it is true and you agree with it - does not make you an advocate for your employees. Helping to identify legitimate problems and helping develop solutions for those problems does make you an advocate - and a valuable supervisor.

Tip #10

Sincere and Specific Appreciation

I believe that appreciation can be the #1 employee performance accelerator - if done correctly. The saying, "What gets rewarded, gets repeated" is generally true. And the reward given is less important than how it is given, and by whom.

I met a high school principal a few years ago who had just been appointed to her new job. The teachers were excited because this individual (task-oriented type A personality) had been a really hardworking teacher. The teachers quickly found out the task-oriented principal seldom had time for casual conversation, or even important school-related discussion. She did try to communicate in teacher meetings, where she would show her appreciation by bringing snacks (she paid for herself), and by bringing trinkets (she bought at the Dollar Store) to give out as prizes. By the way, if you are thinking of doing this – please, save your money. No one needs any more junk from the Dollar Store, and junk does not feel like a "Thank You."

After these meetings, there was no time for discussion about anything. If you talked to the principal in her office, she would unintentionally show you why multi-tasking does not work by talking to you over her shoulder while typing on her computer. You would leave feeling frustrated and disrespected.

At the beginning of one school year, all of the teachers received a computer-generated postcard from the principal that read, "We appreciate all you do for the children." In talking to several teachers, it was clear they did not feel appreciated (and the single generic postcard is not going to fix that). They did not feel appreciated by their boss, who seldom had time to talk to them and who never gave them sincere, specific, or individual appreciation. This task-oriented supervisor could have filled that void by something as simple as placing a sticky note on a teacher's mailbox that said something like, "Peeked in on your English class today. It was great the way you got the kids to interact with you. Nice job."

Examples of inadequate appreciation by supervisors are all around us. It is amazing that something so seemingly simple can sometimes be so difficult. Here are a few thoughts on making your show of appreciation count.

- **Group appreciation.** Group appreciation ("Thanks everyone. Good job today.") is sometimes warranted. While it does not have the same power as individual appreciation, if an event happens where group appreciation should be given and is not, that failure to show appreciation will definitely be noticed. Be aware, however, that sometimes group appreciation feels mechanical to the receiver - like it is a leadership "technique" that you were required to do. This is especially true if most of your feedback prior to that point has been critical or there is a lack of trust between you and your employees. In such cases, group appreciation will not only be ineffective, it may be mocked by some subordinates.

- **Individual appreciation.** An individual show of appreciation always feels more sincere because it is not the norm. Plus, it is about them personally. If my boss went out of his way to thank me personally for a job well done, it is more meaningful, more likely to build trust between myself and my boss, and more likely to get me to repeat the behavior in hopes that I will someday get thanked again. It does not have to be a formal commendation or comments on a performance evaluation either. Individual appreciation can come in the form of a casual face-to-face discussion, an email, a text, or any form of communication.

- **Specifics.** While any appreciation is better than none (usually), telling everyone, "I appreciate all you do for the community" is not likely to get you the results you want. There may be occasions when you do not have specifics to offer but still want to say thanks because you are sincerely appreciative.

Go ahead and show your appreciation. But anytime you can offer specifics, you will not only come across as more sincere to your employees, but it will be more likely that the desired behavior you are commenting on will be repeated.

Take, for example, something as seemingly minor as a report you reviewed. Maybe you occasionally say, "Nice job on that report." It is better than nothing, but will not likely get anything repeated, because the employee does not know what you liked about the report. Consider this alternative, "Nice job on the report. The detailed information you included from that victim was really good and should help close the case. They really appreciated that you called them back and told them what was going on with the case." Simple specifics such as this might get the specific behavior you like repeated. If you want desired behavior repeated, comment on that behavior.

TIP: Appreciation is not always about awards and commendations. Everyone wants appreciation - if it is sincere. No one wants to feel manipulated. And insincere appreciation feels like an attempt at manipulation. Finally, if you want a particular behavior to be repeated, be specific about the behavior you are praising.

Tip #11

Effective Meetings

Meetings can be a great source of information and engagement, or they can be a great source of frustration and a major waste of time. I worked for a boss for a few years who almost never had meetings. I was fine with that because I was task-oriented, self-motivated, and did not like to be micromanaged. If I needed information, I went to him. We worked well together. That boss was replaced by a new boss who liked lots of meetings. So many, in fact, that the staff began to dread all of his meetings and looked for excuses to skip them.

Staff meetings are common, probably necessary, and most organizations have them in some form. That said, few people like staff meetings. Staff members understand they need to go to meetings, but most would like to spend their time on other aspects of the job.

The purpose of a meeting should be to provide up-to-date useful information and not just put bodies in the seat so someone can say they had a staff meeting. There should be a reason for the meeting and a reason why particular individuals are being invited or required to attend. And finally, there should be equal opportunity for information sharing and engagement. Meetings should not be a 60-minute lecture.

Meetings should have a purpose. There should be an agenda for every meeting. Somewhere on the agenda there should be a time slot for the concerns of those in attendance. A little time can be allocated for non-agenda items during this time slot, but do not allow a major focus shift. The purpose here is to engage people while, at the same time, not allowing anyone to capture the focus of the meeting and turn it into a gripe session. But if you do not allow a little time for attendees to speak, some will become totally disengaged until they hear those magic words "The meeting is over."

Here are a few guidelines regarding effective staff meetings:

- **Establish your meeting rules.** People should know what to expect with regards to how you will run your meetings.

- **Set time limits.** Meetings should generally not run longer than 30-60 minutes.

- **No bragging.** If you have nothing to say relevant to the agenda or immediate concerns, then do not speak, brag, tell stories, or ask unrelated questions.

- **No one gets reamed out.** Meetings are for sharing information. If someone needs corrective feedback, it should be done in private and not at a meeting.

- **Missed meetings.** If someone skips a mandatory meeting for an <u>unexcused</u> absence, hold them accountable.

- **No Gripe sessions.** Do not allow comments to escalate into an all-out, all-hands gripe session. For legitimate complaints, determine if the meeting is the appropriate place or if it should be discussed after the meeting in private.

- **No Pile On.** Do not allow people to pile on complaints simply because one person started complaining and the rest feel comfortable piling on. Group venting can increase anger and hurt morale.

- **Extra Communication Source.** Meetings are one method of communication, but should not be your only method.

TIP: Meetings cost valuable time, so make sure the meeting is valuable. Well-run meetings can be a useful source of information and information sharing, but should not be used as a group gripe session.

Tip #12

Career Mentors

Can you recall an individual you worked with who was a positive role model and made sure you chose good career choices? If you were fortunate enough to have that one person – that mentor, you know that employees today could benefit significantly from such a person.

Short-term mentors help new employees. They could be field training officers, experienced employees, or immediate supervisors. They provide routine advice on everything from properly completing assigned tasks to surviving or excelling in the workplace culture.

Long-term mentors deal more with job satisfaction and career issues rather than daily tasks. These career mentors could be the same people as the short-term mentors, but their relationship with the employee is based on more than helping the employee meet the daily minimum acceptable standard. Long-term, or career mentors, are people who have decided they want to invest a part of themselves - something more than the job requires - to helping an employee succeed in their career. It is a form of career guidance based on mutual respect and trust.

New employees are occasionally advised to seek out career mentors and to ask for career guidance that may be outside of formal on-the-job-training procedures. The employee lucky enough to find such a mentor should keep things on a professional level, leave out any workplace drama or gossip, and try to meet a few times each year. While it is great if the employee searches for and actually finds such a mentor, the reality is that few employees will make such an effort often, because they do not realize they should. Sometimes they are afraid of the response, and often for good reason.

I recall once asking a supervisor for some career advice. His response was sarcastic and demoralizing. I regretted asking his advice. In addition, some employees will not go to supervisors for career advice because they are overly concerned about what their peers might think. So while many would like career advice, few actually ask for it. The alternative is for supervisors to proactively seek out mentees.

A word of caution - treating everyone fairly does not mean treating them all the same. It means that everyone that behaves a certain way will get treated exactly the same. I mention this only because it may be painfully obvious that some employees are not deserving of the extra effort it takes for you to be their career mentor. But if you see some spark of enthusiasm, a glimpse of motivation, some indication that a particular employee really cares about the job, and maybe even shows a wisp of future leadership potential, it is probably worth the extra effort and time investment to mentor that employee.

Mentor him, even if he never asks to be mentored, and even if no one gives you a title or a pay increase to go along with your extra efforts. Here is what mentors do:

- **They listen.** Provide advice and encouragement, but listen and understand the employee's situation. What you may have wanted in your career may not be what the employee wants for his career.

- **They are patient.** The employee wants advice and direction. Constructive criticism may even be appropriate. What they do not want is a lecture from a parent.

- **They are role models.** You cannot be a successful mentor unless you set an appropriate example for behavior.

- **They Care.** There is more to mentoring than just doing your job as a supervisor. Mentoring requires more investment in the relationship. You have to care about your mentee to provide advice that is right for that individual.

- **They understand what they get.** A successful mentoring relationship helps not only the employee, but is very satisfying for the mentor. Know that you can make a difference.

- **They understand what the organization gets.** Loyalty, job satisfaction, trust, improved morale, long-term commitment, allies against the organization's morale-killers, and the development of future leaders. Not bad for something that costs nothing but a little bit of your time.

TIP: If you want to improve job satisfaction and organizational commitment - all while developing future leaders - take the time to be a career mentor.

Tip #13

Managing B Players

In an earlier tip I discussed the so-called 10-80-10 theory (or 20-60-20 theory depending on your organization). Your workforce is probably made up of about 10% of self-motivated, ambitious (and sometimes high maintenance) employees at the top. You probably have about 10% at the bottom who you wish would retire or resign. And you probably have 60-80% of your workforce in the middle, who are average employees. We probably will not be able to change the top 10% or bottom 10%. But that bottom group, in particular, is where we tend to spend most of our efforts. In some cases, we all but ignore the middle group.

Let's begin with the stark truth not everyone in the middle group is capable of reaching the top 10%. In addition, some of those employees are capable, but just do not want the challenges or responsibilities associated with getting to the top 10%. Some employees like being what I call our "B Players." Truth be told, we need B Players. We need lots of them. We could not be successful in our leadership efforts without a good core of solid B Players.

Understand that all B Players are not created equal. Here are a few different types of B Players:

The Runner Up. These are B Players who would like to advance, but either do not test or interview well, or things just did not work out like they had hoped. They are solid workers with the desire to advance, but that desire is not always in alignment with ability and opportunity. These employees have a high potential for frustration and may need extra encouragement. Do not make false promises about advancement, but focus on their value to the job.

Former A Players. Some B Players are former A Players. Maybe they had a leadership position or carried a high workload and decided they want to take a step back. Maybe they want a better work-life balance. They may still accept responsibility, but do not seek the daily pressure of being an A Player. These B Players require careful handing, because they may know your job as well you. The good news is that they can sometimes elevate the performance of other B Players.

Silent Experts. Some B Players have become subject matter experts on particular topics. Because they have found a particular niche that interests them, they have pursued formal education or on-the-job training that has made them the go-to person anytime a question on that subject arises. They are generally not seeking advancement, but cherish their role as the (sometimes informal) in-house expert. Silent experts are extremely valuable. If you have one, cultivate that expertise. It will not only serve the organization well, it is the quickest way to guarantee that individual's job satisfaction and organizational commitment.

Under the Radar. Under the radar B Players are those employees, who have chosen not to seek advancement or notoriety, but still are competent in their jobs and have a strong work ethic. They are not risk takers, so are not keen on change. But they are solid performers, doing their job day in and day out without much, if any, complaining. From a supervisor's standpoint, they are low maintenance. A supervisor's biggest mistake with these individuals is thinking they do not need attention because they never complain. As a supervisor, you need to find something other than that big event to show your appreciation because that big event may never happen. Appreciation is one strategy that will help keep this valuable employee around for a long time.

Here are some general guidelines for supervising B Players:

- **Individual Treatment.** B Players generally respond best to individual attention and appreciation from their supervisors. They are typically not seeking the public spotlight.

- **Work-Life Balance.** B Players can usually perform to an A Player level if required for a short time, but have chosen their performance level to reach a desired work-life balance. Do not sell them short because they are trying to achieve that balance.

- **Appreciation.** B Players need appreciation as much as A players. Do not wait for the big event. Show appreciation for their value to the organization, their expertise, their character, and the fact that you count on them as an integral part of the organization.

- **Responsibility.** Whenever possible, give B Players work that makes them feel valued. Find out what your B Player likes to do best at his job and work hard to find a way to occasionally give some of that work to the B Player, so that he knows he is viewed as a valued professional.

TIP: B Players are the core of any successful organization. Help those, who want to advance, achieve that perceived A Player status. For the rest, work hard to keep your solid-performing B Players committed to you and the organization.

Tip #14

Supervisors Appreciating Supervisors

My father once mailed me large envelope full of newspaper clippings he had been saving for many years. Reading through the clippings brought back fond memories of the early part of my career. It is nice to see your name in print for doing a good job. There were news articles that mentioned how I recovered stolen cars, solved burglaries, worked during a hurricane, established a crime scene unit, and solved a major antique theft to list just a few. There were even two articles (about 8 years apart) about ride-a-longs reporters did with me as I explained my law enforcement duties. I found a couple articles that mentioned my appointment as a police chief in another community and a few articles about the beginning of my tenure as chief. Then there seemed to be a noticeable absence of newspaper clippings.

 I called my father and asked, "How come you did not keep any of the more recent articles when I was chief?" He said, "Because when you were a patrolman and a sergeant, the articles were about the good things you did. When you were chief, the articles were about you telling the media about the good things other people did. The articles weren't really about you."

What my father said was true. It struck me that sometimes as we rise in rank or position, the good things we do are not always newsworthy events. As important as good leadership is to your organization's success, good leadership stories probably will not make the local paper. For younger employees, honorable mention in those news articles is a form of recognition. In my case, those articles made me proud, and I felt more motivated. If there was an article in the paper about me recovering several stolen cars, you better believe that when the next stolen motor vehicle report came in that I was on the hunt trying to be the officer who found that car and made the arrest. What gets rewarded (or recognized) gets repeated!

Recognition and rewards can come in the form of a formal commendation, a newspaper article, or just a supervisor telling you that you did a good job. Now imagine for a moment you are in a position where your local paper does not report on any of your good leadership efforts or results. Good leadership practices are not as exciting to a readership as the day's next big crime story. Good leadership stories almost never make the local paper (unfortunately the bad leadership stories do). Good leadership results probably will not get a formal commendation either. And sadly, while most supervisors today realize the importance of showing appreciation to their subordinates, occasionally people who supervise other supervisors sometimes forget that what gets rewarded or recognized gets repeated.

If you manage or supervise other supervisors, please understand that your subordinate supervisors like to be appreciated and/or recognized for their good work every bit as much as non-supervisory personnel. Wouldn't it be nice if some of those nice things that are occasionally said at a supervisor's retirement party were actually said throughout the supervisor's career? We all work for someone. Almost everyone has a supervisor or a boss. And we all like appreciation and recognition. It lets us know we are doing a good job.

Here as some ideas for showing appreciation to the supervisors that you supervise.

- **Be specific.** Tell them occasionally what they are doing right. Do not generalize. Saying "You're doing a good job." is not as helpful as making a comment about specific behavior. After a supervisor handles a difficult employee situation or calms down an angry employee, the supervisor's supervisor might say something like, "The way you calmed him down was amazing. I wish more of my supervisors had your communication skills." If you appreciate your supervisor's professionalism, tell him what about that professionalism you really like or respect the most.

- **Spend some quality time.** Call the supervisor into the office occasionally just to ask how things are going. Make comments of your observations of the good work you have seen him doing. It should not be all about statistics being done by his subordinates. The positive discussion should be about what you see that you like. By the way, if you want to criticize because you do not like the way something is being done, do that at a separate meeting. Do not spoil positive interaction with negative feedback, and do not water down negative feedback by adding a couple good guy comments to soften the blow.

- **Do not make them guess.** Supervisors should not have to guess how they are doing. Results are not always obvious. Neither supervisors nor anyone else should be surprised at performance evaluation time - even for good things. If you like something you see in a supervisor - the way he talks to people in general, his calmness in difficult situations, his character, work ethic, or integrity - say something.

TIP: The adage "What gets rewarded or recognized gets repeated" works as well for supervisors as anyone else. If one of your supervisors is doing a good job, let him know specifically what you like about what he is doing.

Tip #15

Unappreciated Appreciation

It is hard to imagine someone not appreciating their boss showing them appreciation or recognition for good work or accomplishments on the job. The first time I observed someone overtly showing his disdain (or at least what he wanted to convey as distain) for such recognition was about 30 years ago. I was a relatively new employee in an organization with a very structured commendation program. Commendations were given out once a year at a ceremony preceding the town's Memorial Day parade, after which you were required to march in the parade. It was clear to me that some coworkers were not happy about marching in the parade and claimed to not care about the commendations. The more vocal complainers were also the organization's chronically negative employees. I recall one in particular who was extremely moody and unpredictable.

 The Chief, to his credit, worked hard to try to find ways to recognize as many people as possible at the awards ceremony. In retrospect, I think he erred only in believing that the negative attitudes of some employees might change by giving them marginally deserved commendations. At one such annual ceremony, the aforementioned moody employee received a commendation for some insignificant effort on his part. When the ceremony ended, I watched in disbelief as he took his commendation and put it through the shredder.

I had almost forgotten about that incident until recently when a police captain asked me what to do about an employee that refused a commendation. He said one of his employees (who had a history of having a negative attitude) had been given a commendation at their awards ceremony, and gave it back to him saying he did not want the award and refused to accept it. The captain said in addition to that incident, he had been personally trying to show his appreciation to his employees by sending them emails telling them whenever they had done a good job. He said the Union requested that he stop sending those emails to the employees.

We can never be certain of why a particular employee reacts as those did in these examples. One thing seems obvious and that is the employees mentioned were probably angry. They intentionally acted out in a way that was designed to anger, or at least hurt the feelings of, the person who made the effort to award the commendation. Rather than being so passive-aggressive, a more mature individual might have kept the commendation but communicated why he was angry to his boss. It has been said that maturity does not always come with age. Sometimes age comes alone.

If someone refuses a commendation or tells you they do not want your "good guy" emails, they are sending you a message. Such resistance is extremely frustrating because showing appreciation is not always easy. Sometimes that apparent lack of appreciation by subordinates who receive our recognition makes leaders want to stop these well-intentioned efforts. It is unfortunate that the negativity of one person or a small group of persons overshadows all the good that comes from these efforts. If you encounter employees like this, please keep in mind the following:

- **Everyone wants to be appreciated.** Good employees, obviously, want to be appreciated. Even negative employees want to know they are valued. They may never admit to wanting your appreciation, but healthy adults want to make a difference. And we occasionally need someone to tell us that we are making that difference.

- **Trust is crucial.** Some employees see formal awards ceremonies as a technique by their bosses to make the boss look good. This is especially true if the employee does not trust his supervisor. If an employee perceives he has been unjustly treated by the boss or the organization, he may feel management is trying to manipulate him with a commendation while ignoring other issues. Apathy about commendations has more to do with the working relationship than it does with the commendation.

- **Good work deserves recognition (even by those who do not want it).** If you are giving recognition or commendations to those who deserve it, then it does not really matter if they want it or think such gestures are silly. We show appreciation because it is the right thing to do. Whether he chooses to frame his commendation or throw it in the trash does not change the fact that he deserved the recognition.

- **Look deeper.** If they refuse an award or say they no longer want to be told they are doing a good job, look deeper. There are unresolved issues. If the union does not want you to recognize good work, too bad. They do not get to make that call. If an individual tells you not to recognize his good work, there is a reason and the reason has to do with the work relationship. It is really all about trust, and you need to find out why he has lost trust in you or the organization.

TIP: We show appreciation and give recognition for good work because it is the right thing to do. The fact that it improves performance is a side benefit. Do not stop doing it because an individual or the union does not appear to appreciate the appreciation.

Tip #16

Working With Extroverts

No one is entirely introverted or extroverted, but those employees who appear to be on the extremes of either can become a challenge for supervisors. For example, one supervisor recently told me he was having a problem with an overly talkative employee. I had mentioned the importance of connecting with our employees through casual conversation. The supervisor said that his problem was not getting this particular employee to talk, but getting him to stop talking. He said the employee would sometimes come to his office and talk about everything from his daughter's soccer game the night before to the new idea he had that would help save the department money and raise morale. He said the employee wasn't necessarily complaining about anything, but was more or less saying whatever was on his mind at that moment. The supervisor said the employee had great charisma and confidence, but the long conversations were starting to interfere with work (both the supervisor's and the employee's) because they were so time consuming.

Extroverts can be friendly, funny, and make work enjoyable, but they can also be aggravating. You may wish you could flip a switch and turn them off – or at least tone them down. If they come up with an idea, they will be happy to share it with you. As they talk about the idea, they will often think of new ideas or improvements to their old ideas. They tend to think out loud, so do not automatically accept their first idea as their finished product or thought. They are often plentiful on concepts, but sometimes lacking on details. If they come up with an idea you think has merit, you will need to help them flush out the details by asking detail-oriented questions.

Managing extroverts requires more face time than managing introverts. Extroverts would not survive well in a workplace where the only communication from their supervisor was an occasional email. They need to be around people to bounce ideas and thoughts off of others. They thrive in a social work environment and are energized by external stimuli such as committees, group assignments, and interaction with their supervisors and the public.

Author Fran Leibowitz said, "The opposite of talking is not listening. The opposite of talking is waiting." This is an accurate statement for many extroverts. Sometimes they are so impatient waiting for someone to finish a thought that they will interrupt and finish the statement for them. Unfortunately, sometimes they are wrong in their premature conclusions.

Here are some suggestions for supervising extroverts:

- **Allow them face time.** They need interaction with their supervisors. Let them know how they are doing. Ask them for ideas (and details of those ideas). They will always do better with in-person contacts than with electronic communication.

- **Coach them on listening.** If they start interrupting, or inserting their own comments or conclusions before others finish, let them know that it is not generally appreciated by anyone (including you).

- **Leading is not dominating.** Extroverts assigned to a group will typically try to lead any group effort. Make sure others do not allow the extrovert to dominate to the point that the group shuts down and the extrovert's word automatically becomes the group's word.

- **Non-verbal caution.** Most extroverts respond to non-verbal cues and are adapt at reading body language. Be careful about showing your frustration in facial expressions or tone of voice.

- **Manage at meetings.** Extroverts tend to talk at meetings more than others. You can ask them to "hold that thought" because of time. You can also say you want to hear from someone you have not heard from yet. Be assertive to prevent them from controlling your meeting. Take a break if necessary and give them honest feedback in private. Let them know you value their contribution, but you need to hear from others as well.

- **Your time is important.** Making connections with employees is important, and casual conversations are a great way to make connections. But do not allow the extrovert to abuse that concept by engaging in never-ending casual conversations that prevent him (and you) from doing the work you were hired to perform. Have conversations. But at the appropriate time, shift the focus back to work.

TIP: Extroverts can be gifted talkers and have an abundance of ideas. Use their strengths, but manage their weaknesses. Do not allow them to dominate all of your time, or to smother the ideas of other valuable (but less talkative) employees.

Tip #17

Saboteurs

Have you had a new subordinate or coworker who, when you met him, came across as your biggest fan? They seemed to admire you, respect you, and make you feel that you had value and purpose in the organization. Maybe that subordinate even praised your hard work.

Hearing such praise, you might begin to feel pretty smug about your great leadership abilities. And then it happens - that first clue that something is not quite right. Maybe you think you overheard that person talking about you in a negative way to his peers (or worse - to your boss), but you are not quite sure. Maybe you thought you saw him roll his eyes when you made a comment, or maybe he made a snide remark to get a laugh from coworkers after you made an opening statement at a meeting.

When questioned by you, this employee professes undying loyalty and admiration for you, as well as shock that you would think he would ever talk bad about you. Then several coworkers, whose opinions you trust, approach you and advise you to watch yourself with regards to the employee. Are they right or are they just jockeying for favored status themselves?

Could it be that you have been duped by the organization's backstabber - The Saboteur? You want to think the best of people, but if clues start piling up that an employee may be a saboteur, it would be a mistake to ignore those clues indefinitely. If gushing admiration and backstabbing, undermining behavior seems to reside in the same person, you are likely being manipulated.

Saboteurs can be dangerous to your career, and you will not likely be able to control all of their behavior, but you can control your reaction to their behavior. Here are some simple guidelines that might help.

- **Do not be hypersensitive.** Not everyone who compliments you has an agenda. Maybe they trust and respect you, or your personalities mesh. But if their show of admiration is combined with backstabbing behavior, proceed with caution.

- **Do not be in denial.** It is good to think positive, but if backstabbing behavior appears obvious to everyone but you, listen to trusted input. Anyone can be fooled by a manipulative saboteur.

- **Do not try to change him.** It is not likely that you will change a saboteur. His behavior may be related to his personality, which you cannot change. His impression management techniques have probably been working for him for years.

- **Do not become obsessed.** The anger and frustration caused by a saboteur can turn to physical reactions like headaches, heartburn, and anxiety.

- **Do not give anyone that much power over you.** He is only one employee. You have others who need a good leader and role model. Do not start treating others differently just because you've discovered a saboteur in the ranks.

- **Assessment and Response.** Gather accurate information. List situations where you feel your leadership, work, or reputation has been undermined or sabotaged by this person. Awareness of minor situations can help you maintain a perspective about the employee, but require no action on your part. If you do decide to act, do not make any decisions regarding the individual when you are angry. Your goal is not to engage in endless debate, but rather to make him aware of your perception of the situation, and your expectations for the future.

TIP: Saboteurs are a fact of life. Do not let them negatively impact your job performance, your confidence, your enthusiasm, or your treatment of others. React when appropriate in a calm manner that will best serve your career and the organization.

Tip #18

Telephone Basics

People who encounter anyone in your organization for the first time take about seven seconds to form an opinion about your organization. Unfortunately, that first encounter is not always with a person skilled in phone etiquette. It could be a person who seldom answers the phone, or it could be your most abrasive employee. It could also be you while you are busy doing a dozen other things at the same time. In those seven seconds, that caller makes a determination as to whether they like, dislike, or are indifferent towards your organization. That is the whole organization and most everyone in it, not just the person answering the phone. Unfair, I know, but that is the facts of life when dealing with the public.

In many cases, the only chance your organization will have to make a good first impression will be on the telephone. Listed below are some telephone basics that should apply to all supervisors, as well as those who answer the phone as part of their job.

- **Rings.** Try to answer your phone within two or three rings. If the phone rings numerous times, the caller is wondering why no one is answering. They will not automatically assume you are busy.

- **Scripts.** Use a script to get everyone to answer the phone the same way. The script should include the name of the organization, the name of the person who is answering the phone, and "How may I help you?"

- **Hold.** Take ownership of the call. Do not just hit the hold button without knowing who it is or why they are calling. Assure the caller someone will be with them shortly, and give a time expectation if possible. Transfer as much information as possible with the call so the exact questions are not repeated.

- **Transfers.** If you are going to transfer the call, take the basic info and then advise the caller you will be transferring them to a person who is better suited to handle that situation. Do not make the caller tell you a lengthy story just because you are curious.

- **What callers want?** All any caller wants is no hassle. They want someone to listen to their problem or situation. They want some verbal feedback from someone in your organization. Using the name of the caller while talking helps create a perception that the caller is being listened to.

- **Taking Messages.** When taking a call for someone else, act as if every call is critical. It just may be. Be as specific as possible about a return date and time of the person they are trying to reach, but do not promise a call back time. Offer to help if the caller would like to talk to you.

- **Do not provide personal information.** Do not tell the caller that the person they want is "in the bathroom," or "I do not know where he is." All that is required is to say that "He is tied up at the moment, but I will give him the message that you called, and he will call you back as soon as he can."

- **Call Screeners.** Sometimes the call is of a personal nature. Callers should not be forced to give more than a brief explanation to the screener. If the person is busy, the screener should take a message. The screener can also provide options (i.e. "He is on the other line right now. Is there something I could help you with? I can take a message or transfer you to his voice mail.") People who have options tend to get less angry.

TIP: A few minutes of applying good phone skills by both supervisors and subordinates now can save hours later trying to apologize or convince a caller of the good intentions of the organization.

Tip #19

Think They Know It All People

Maybe you have had the frustrating experience of working with someone who always seems to be right and wants everyone to know he is the smartest person in the room. Even more frustrating is the person who thinks he knows it all - but clearly does not. This person wastes valuable time at meetings by providing useless and often wrong information, or seemingly crazy ideas. They try to force their way into every conversation, often by providing pointless comments that may have nothing to do with the conversation. And like so many other problem employees, they do not take subtle hints. People laugh at them, ignore their ideas, even point out that they are wrong, all of which only seems to strengthen their resolve to show how smart they are while getting some attention in the process.

"Think they know it all's" are people-focused employees. They seldom have any evil intent. They are motivated by a strong desire to seek attention. They seek attention by making comments of questionable accuracy, or by providing ideas that have not been well-thought out in hopes of getting the recognition they so desperately need. Sometimes these employees sound believable, which can cause problems if the bad idea is followed by other employees. Typically, however, they are ignored most of the time, which means good ideas are thrown out with the bad, regardless of their merit.

Here are a few thoughts for dealing with your "thinks he knows it all" person:

- **Recognize intent over content.** In meetings, you can thank him for contributing rather than arguing about what you have determined is a ridiculous suggestion or idea. For those seeking attention, this may satisfy their appetite at least temporarily.

- **Does it really matter?** Pick and choose your battles. If what they are saying is simply an annoyance and will not matter tomorrow or next week, sometimes it may be better to ignore the comment than embarrass the person – which, in any case, will not change their personality.

- **Get specifics.** They love to talk in generalities. If you are discussing an important issue and they are injecting ideas or alleged facts about which you are doubtful, ask for specifics. Try to come across as being curious, rather than appearing that you want to prove them wrong to embarrass them.

- **Facts are facts.** If they are providing information you know to be false, and that information could be harmful to your employees or the organization, you have a duty to provide accurate information. To counteract a false statement, you could say something like, "That is an interesting point, but from what I read in (insert the appropriate documentation source), I believe..."

- **Private Feedback.** If the behavior becomes a problem, counseling is warranted. Let him know the consequences of the behavior which could include the fact that no one wants to attend a meeting with him or bring up anything at the meeting for fear he will go off on a time-wasting tangent. Let him know what your expectations are for the future.

- **Catch him doing something right.** Since this person is more focused on getting attention than many other employees, sometimes supervisors need to work a little harder to catch him doing something right.

TIP: "Think They Know It All" people are focused on getting attention, even if they look foolish in the process. Make corrections on important topics with supported facts while working hard to avoid embarrassing the individual - and then catch him doing something right.

Tip #20

Imposter Syndrome

Have you ever heard that voice in your head that challenged your worthiness for your current leadership position? Maybe it is that tiny, yet nagging, voice that says, "Maybe today is the day they find out I should not be here. Maybe I do not deserve this position." That little voice in your head can cause you to waste valuable time and make bad decisions that will make others begin to wonder if maybe you are not qualified for the position. Confidence in our ability generally comes with time on the job, but even the best leaders, the best authors, the best musicians, and the greatest athletes all have moments when they feel they do not deserve the position or status they have achieved. It is called the *Imposter Syndrome*.

    The *Imposter Syndrome* affects high achievers, including those in leadership positions. It happens when leaders are unable to recognize their own accomplishments. Despite abundant evidence of their competence, these leaders are convinced that they are not ready for the position they hold and will soon be discovered as frauds. In reality, most of us never feel we are really ready for our leadership position regardless of our experience or education. When we get the job, we sometimes dismiss it as luck, or we somehow fooled others into believing we are more capable than we really are.

Listening too intently to those voices of self-doubt and letting the *Imposter Syndrome* run wild in your head will cause several problems:

1. You end up working harder, and spending more hours at work than you should while trying to prove you deserve the position. This puts a strain on coworkers and our family.

2. You sometimes neglect important new tasks by staying busy doing only the tasks you are really good at because you do not want anyone to see your failure at something you are not yet experienced in.

3. You spend more time than you should doing parts of your old job, where you were comfortable, and less time addressing new challenges that are essential responsibilities of your new position.

These factors, if not recognized, can cause leaders to work too hard at the wrong things and turn the *Imposter Syndrome* into a self-fulling prophecy whereby subordinates begin to believe that you are not qualified for the job. In addition to understanding that almost all leaders experience the *Imposter Syndrome* to some degree at various points in their career, here are a few suggestions to help you work through those self-doubts.

- **Comparisons.** The *Imposter Syndrome* exists because you are comparing yourself to some perfect ideal of a leader that never actually existed.

- **Look at your past success.** Sometimes you may need to look at your own resume for reassurance. You make a difference in the lives of others, but sometimes we all need to be reminded of that fact.

- **Understand it for what it is.** *Imposter Syndrome* is a common occurrence in high achievers. If you feel it, consider yourself a high achiever.

- **Mistakes happen.** Making occasional mistakes does not mean you are not qualified for the job, it just means you are human.

TIP: Good leadership does not require that you are always the hardest worker or smartest employee. Good leadership, however, does require that you work through your doubts to continue to develop your leadership skills for the benefit of your employees and the organization.

Tip #21

Overly Sensitive Employees

I once had an administrative assistant who was extremely moody, and seemed bored, depressed, and angry, among a host of other emotions. If I even hinted that the work being done was insufficient, everyone who came in contact with her would be subjected to her emotional displays. I was unhappy with almost every aspect of her work, and yet I normally remained silent, wishing the problem would fix itself. Only my occasional anger would motivate me to deal directly with the problem. But then afterwards, I would have to deal with her emotional fallout.

The conflict avoidance I engaged in at that stage of my career certainly had a lot to do with my inexperience, but it also had a lot to do with this particular employee being overly sensitive to even the tiniest hint of criticism. Tears, anger, the silent treatment towards me, unpleasantness towards others, and complaining to everyone who would listen, occurred far too often whenever she received constructive feedback from any supervisor.

The tenure of this employee ended only when she resigned over a perceived injustice. While my inexperience had caused me to ignore the problem for far too long, I learned a lot about the need for assertiveness from that experience. Actually, my assertiveness kicked in two days after she had a tantrum and resigned when she called asking for her old job back. Not a chance!

From this experience, I also learned that I did not have to endure unacceptable behavior just because an employee is overly sensitive to criticism. Unacceptable behavior is unacceptable behavior. It will not go away by itself. It needs to be brought to the employee's attention – even if they are overly sensitive. The way we confront that employee may require a little more planning, but our interaction should still be based on being assertive, rather than avoiding the conflict. Here are some guidelines for dealing with the overly sensitive employee:

- **Have a plan.** Just winging it for these employees usually does not work. Figure out what you want to say and how you want to say it in advance. Even consider scripting out your conversation. You do not have to read the script, but it will help you present your thoughts in an orderly (and sensitive) manner.

- **Do not be too brief.** When providing feedback to most employees, your responses can often be direct and to the point. For the overly sensitive employee, you can be assertive, but do not be too direct or it may feel harsh and uncaring to this employee.

- **Fill in the gaps.** Some overly sensitive employees are good at, or at least think they are good at, reading people. If you do not fully explain your criticism or suggestion, they will fill in the blanks with their own perceptions which may or may not be correct.

- **Skip the tough love.** Do not try to toughen these employees by being too harsh or direct. You will not be able to change their personality style by crashing head-first into it.

- **Do not walk on eggshells.** While it is true these employees may be more sensitive than others to criticism, supervisors do not do them or the organization any justice by ignoring bad behavior in hopes of avoiding conflict.

- **Do not force conversations.** If you provide feedback and it is not well received, conversation may be helpful, but should not be forced. If the employee says he needs time to think, do not force conversations or even handshakes at that particular moment.

- **Small doses work best.** Feedback in small doses work best for highly sensitive employees. Do not wait until you have a long list before bringing it to the attention of the employee. If you provide a laundry list of complaints, you will lose their attention. Keep the feedback narrow in scope.

- **Criticize the behavior and not the person.** This is especially true for sensitive employees. Sensitive employees are good at hearing the distinction. Be careful not to judge the person or the personality. You are not likely to change personality. If you are unhappy with behavior, it is your job to change it until it reaches an acceptable standard.

TIP: All employees are different, and some are more sensitive to real or imagined criticism than others. You will not be able to avoid conflict entirely with the underperforming but overly sensitive employee. But you can plan your feedback to not only change behavior but to minimize a negative emotional response.

Tip #22

Ownership Psychology

Usually, when I read about employee ownership, it is in a positive context with the thought that if we can get our employees to take ownership in their duties and responsibilities, they will be more committed to the organization's mission. That is probably true in most cases, and working towards that ownership mentality usually generates positive results and improved performance. Nevertheless, there is a potential downside to the ownership mindset. Psychological ownership is the feeling of possessiveness and of being psychologically tied to an object (or the way something is done) with the result that the object (or procedure) is considered part of the employee. This can make change difficult.

    A historical tourist attraction in the northeast recently experienced some financial difficulties. The 18th century fort was rich in history and was generally loved by history enthusiasts, tourists, historical reenactors, and locals. Many of the reenactors and locals felt it was "their fort." The fort is privately owned by a non-profit organization, and when the financial future began to look bleak, management was changed.

The new director immediately made changes that included limiting the number of reenactments, as well as which groups would be invited to participate. Local residents were no longer given free admission – a privilege they had enjoyed for about 20 years. Reenactment groups started boycotting the fort, locals voiced their displeasure to the media, and everyone thought the new director would be replaced. It seemed the only people not upset were the board of directors, who for the first time in a decade, were seeing a profit at the fort. As aggravating as the changes were to the many who felt a loss of ownership in the fort, the changes were needed if the fort was to survive.

The fort made the right changes for its long-term financial stability. Could they have done a better job at including committed volunteers, reenactors, and locals in their decision-making process? I think so. Their failure in this regard made the changes hard to swallow. These same issues with change can occur on a smaller scale in any organization. Here are points to consider:

- **Additive Change.** If a person believes they are gaining something by change, they are more open to accepting the change. Additive change does not have to be material items. It could be as simple as allowing employee input into the proposed change. If employees feel like they are part of the process, it is more likely that the change will succeed.

- **Subtractive change.** If a person feels they are losing something as a result of the change, they will be highly resistant to the change. This could be a material loss or a loss of control or influence. Employees who feel this loss will become significant resistors to proposed changes.

- What is in the best interest of the organization is not always sufficient to convince an employee that there is a benefit to the change.

- The fact that an employee has no legitimate ownership does not minimize the feeling of ownership developed over a period of years.

- Management encourages a feeling of ownership to improve commitment. Therefore, management should understand the importance of ownership when it proposes a change to the status quo.

TIP: Psychological ownership is generally a positive factor. And employees who feel ownership are typically more committed to the organization and more self-fulfilled. However, when that perceived ownership is challenged as a result of a proposed change, expect resistance unless you factor in "Additive Change" into your strategy allowing for a new/different sense of ownership by the employee.

Tip #24

The Disgruntled Employee

There have always been and probably always will be disgruntled employees. They run the gamut from the guy who whines a little about every change, or perceived injustice, to the much more serious disgruntled employee - those who commit workplace violence. Some disgruntled employees seem to take issue with almost every coworker, most, if not all, of his supervisors, and seemingly every aspect of the job. Despite your best efforts to continually do what is right for all of your employees, this one employee is convinced he is being unfairly treated – even by you.

If you work in an organization with a union, you might think this disgruntled employee - if he were a union member - has the backing of all other union members. But such employees can cause friction even in their own groups. It seems those same disgruntled employees who cause problems for their supervisors are often just as unhappy with their union stewards, officers, and labor organizers.

The International Association of Machinists and Aerospace Workers, in an article titled *Representing Difficult Members,* mentioned how contract misinterpretations and thoughtless supervisors created lots of work for union stewards. But the article acknowledged that some of the stewards' greatest frustrations and most difficult problems came, not from management, but from their own members. According to the article, these members make impossible demands on the union, get angry when their demands are not met, and do little to help themselves. Sound familiar?

When it comes to these unhappy souls whom you can never satisfy, you should know that it is not really about you (or unions). It is about them. It is who they are with everyone from their immediate supervisor to the union steward trying to help them. So what do the unions tell their stewards to do with these people? Here are a few tips that union officials have offered their stewards. These tips are appropriate for all supervisors dealing with disgruntled employees in union or non-union organizations.

- Do not be too quick to write them off as a chronic complainer not worthy of your time. Sometimes even chronic complainers have legitimate complaints that should be addressed.

- Your response to their visible anger should be calm. Do not start off by defending yourself or the organization. Just listen. Arguing or defensive postures at the outset typically escalate the situation.

- Remain neutral, but interested. Empathetic and uninterrupted listening allows the person to initially have their say. Work to get the person to calm down, so logic overcomes emotion.

- Do not take sides. If the complaint is about a coworker or another supervisor, avoid choosing sides. The focus should be on understanding the issues and what, if anything, can or should be done.

- If the complaint is about you, provide the employee with your interpretation of the situation, which was based on the information available to you at the time you made the decision or took the action.

- After hearing the complaint and probing for clarity, defend the organization, other supervisors, or yourself when appropriate. At the same time, respect the employee's feelings and experiences that may have led to their perceptions.

TIP: Despite the efforts of great leaders, disgruntled employees exist in every organization. Your response to their complaints must not be based on emotions or personalities. It should be based on determining if a legitimate problem exists, and then working on the best short-term and long-term solutions for both the employee and the organization.

Tip #24

Cultivating Ideas

It would be a mistake to assume that the only good ideas come from the people at the top of any organization. While executives, managers, and supervisors have plenty of good ideas, they are certainly not the sole source for innovative thought. In many cases, the non-supervisory employee out in the field doing the job day-in and day-out is in a perfect position to evaluate his or her situation and come up with an idea that may benefit the entire organization. If we can find a way to cultivate these ideas, we might not only make improvements in effectiveness and efficiency and raise customer (public) satisfaction, we could potentially improve employee morale and performance as well.

One of the factors leading to improved morale is job satisfaction, and one of the main elements of job satisfaction is that employees feel valued. What better way to engage with an employee and let them know they are valued than to listen to and, in some cases, implement their ideas?

This strategy, however, is not without challenges. First, we must find a way to encourage idea development at every level. Second, employees have to trust us enough to bring those ideas forward. Third, we must be willing to accept or, at least, test out some ideas regardless of their source. And finally, we have to find a tactful way to say "No thanks." Based on my experience, saying "Thanks for the input" - when an employee promotes an idea that you think is ill conceived - will likely get you an angry employee who will refuse to offer any more ideas. After one such mistake on my part, I knew I needed to find a better way of cultivating ideas while, at the same time, finding a way of declining really bad ideas without demotivating the individual. Here's what my research found:

- Suggestion boxes are more likely to be anonymous complaint boxes than true idea cultivators.

- Staff meetings are not necessarily the best source of innovation. The most talkative employees are not necessarily those with the best ideas. All individuals should be encouraged to develop ideas.

- Let employees know that ideas do not have to be fully developed or perfect. Quantity, creativity, and innovation are more important in the beginning.

- Employees should know in advance that you want to hear all ideas, but that does not mean every idea will be or can be implemented.

- If the idea has no negative impact on the budget, might improve efficiency, or has the potential to make the employee feel encouraged to submit more ideas, consider implementing the idea.

- While actively listening to the idea, ask lots of questions. How did he develop the idea, and how would it be implemented? Not only does this show interest and fleshes out the idea's concept, but sometimes facts surface that enable the idea giver to realize the idea will not work.

- Try to find a way to say "yes." Oftentimes you may not like an employee's idea at first glance, but with just a little modification the concept might work.

- Sometimes it is not a bad idea, just bad timing. Ideas with merit that are not able to be implemented immediately can be tabled for consideration.

- If you say no, or choose to not even test the idea, provide a legitimate reason or explanation (too costly, we do not have the manpower, etc.).

TIP: Continuously cultivate new ideas from all employees. New ideas that originate with individual employees result in improved employee job satisfaction and morale.

Ronald C. Glidden

Tip #25

Limitations of the Written Word

I was at the post office recently and met a high school teacher I had known for many years. It was the end of summer so I asked him if he was looking forward to the start of school. I got grumble in response. He was reading a letter he had just received, and he had the look of anguish on his face. "Trouble?" I asked. He said, "It is from the school." By the look on his face, I thought maybe his employment had been terminated. "Everything all right?" I asked. He replied, "It is from the new principal. Same old BS." He began reading parts of the letter out loud.

"The path to success is paved with the stones of teamwork and pride. These traits are the pillars that will support the weight of our hard work. Working together with a unified vision will allow us to attain our ultimate goal of increasing student achievement."

When the teacher paused to take a breath, the post office lady who was listening said, "I want to gag." The post office lady and I laughed. The teacher did not. I said to the teacher, "I don't see the problem." He said, "The problem is we get one of these form letters every year." He said the letters typically mention how important the "team" is to the success of the students. He said the letters typically include some teamwork-related quotes. But he said the real problem is that in his 20 years at this school, working for eight different principals, he could not recall one administrator ever asking him personally how he was doing. He said not once has any of them ever asked if there was anything they could do that would help him do his job.

If you were not employed in that particular school, the letter would appear to be well meaning. To me, it seemed like an attempt from a new boss to reach out to employees he had not met yet in person. But for those employees at that school who have worked through frequent changes in leadership and equally frequent periods of low morale, they put their own spin on the meaning of the letter.

The written word, either in the form of a letter, a memo, or an email, can quickly reach numerous employees. How that written word is interpreted, however, has as much - if not more - to do with the employee's work environment and the employee's individual history in the organization than it does with the actual written words or the writer's intent. While the written word is extremely important (and useful) for any supervisor, it is not without its limitations or problems. Consider the following:

- Letters, memos, emails, and all formal correspondence written to a group audience will likely be interpreted differently by individuals, depending on their history in the organization.

- The written word is useful for positive feedback or neutral information. One can never have too many communication sources. Refrain from criticism or corrective feedback in group letters.

- Do not go crazy in your written communication with feel-good or witty quotes about teamwork that could have come from the inspirational poster hanging in your office. It can make written correspondence sound insincere.

- Written correspondence should not be the end-all of engagement if you want to connect with your employees and earn their trust. It is a supplemental form of communication. It may be informational, but not necessarily engaging.

- Communication and information can come from many sources. But true employee engagement happens when supervisors communicate in-person, individually, with their employees.

TIPS: Written communication is a valuable form of communication, but it should never be the only form of communication. If you want to show employees you care, do not tell them in a letter. Show them by engaging with them as individuals on a regular basis.

Tip #26

Not Funny

Job related humor can build camaraderie, raise spirits, and help us get through difficult days. Unfortunately, there are supervisors who do not understand there is a difference between humor and unprofessional behavior.

Some professional comedians make us laugh using either self-deprecating humor or generalized humor that does not target a specific person or group. Other professional comedians are opportunists. They make fun of anyone for a laugh. If you are sitting in the audience of an opportunist, you think he is funny, but you always have an uneasy feeling because you hope he does not decide to target you. Imagine working for an opportunist comedian? Funny - when he is making fun of someone else - but you walk around hoping today is not the day he tries to embarrass you for a laugh.

I have observed supervisors who were very funny people and used their humor to make their employees feel good. They make work fun and make their employees look forward to going to work. But I have also observed supervisors who were funny in a different kind of way. They demeaned their subordinates, just to get a laugh.

When that occurs, you can never be sure if the comments are intended to be humorous or hurtful. One thing is for sure – that kind of humor can come at a price. The price paid is often a loss of trust.

Here are just a few examples of humor that resulted in withdrawals of trust from a supervisor's trust account:

- A supervisor engages in sexually explicit humor with a female employee who did not appear offended, until a joke is made about her weight. A complaint is filed and an internal investigation revealed inappropriate sexual humor and workplace harassment. A media frenzy, a lawsuit, discipline, and department-wide sensitivity training follow.

- A supervisor makes jokes about body parts to a female subordinate. Both laugh and joke about the subject. The female subordinate is disciplined months later for an unrelated matter. The previous "humor" is raised as an allegation of sexual harassment. A lawsuit, investigation, media frenzy, and discipline for the supervisor follow.

- A long time police academy instructor makes inappropriate jokes to recruits. On at least one occasion, the instructor gets behind the recruit and makes a sexual gesture. Everyone laughs. The recruit eventually gets disciplined for an unrelated matter. The instructor's previous inappropriate humor is reported, and the whole recruit class comes to the aid of their fellow recruit. A lawsuit, investigation, media frenzy, and discipline - for all of the instructors present during the incident - follow.

- A supervisor continually makes jokes in front of subordinates about how stupid a particular employee is. Everyone laughs, including the targeted employee. But as a result of the constant demeaning humor, the employee's motivation, morale, and work quality suffer. The employee's trust for, and commitment to, that supervisor is nonexistent.

- A chief uses inappropriate humor at every opportunity. It appears the comments are intended to put employees down and embarrass them. The employees become unified in their lack of respect for a boss who rules by fear, intimidation, and his special brand of demeaning humor. The employees collectively report the incidents, and the chief is forced to resign.

It is not that we cannot or should not be funny or have fun at work. It is that as supervisors, we cannot afford to get a laugh at the expense of those we supervise. For those well-meaning supervisors who use all forms of humor and do not realize the risks of inappropriate humor, it is never too late to become more professional. For those who manage by fear and intimation, or who use put-downs to compensate for their own insecurity, you are not reading this anyway. For the rest of us, we sometimes need to be reminded of the following:

- Verbal abuse is not funny, especially if you are the receiver.

- Just because subordinates laugh does not mean they think it is funny, appropriate, or professional.

- For those who consider the consequences of inappropriate humor, know that those consequences can run from a loss of employee trust to lawsuits and discipline, including termination.

- For long-time employees, know that what might have seemed funny to subordinates 20 years ago could get you fired today. As a side note – it was not appropriate 20 years ago either.

- What you say matters. If you are a supervisor, people are listening. What you say helps them form an opinion about your trustworthiness and professionalism.

TIP: We do not have the right to make ourselves look humorous and witty by generating laughs at the expense of our employees.

Tip #27

Hobby Time

I first heard about the importance of a balanced lifestyle many years ago from Dr. Kevin Gilmartin. In his book, *Emotional Survival for Law Enforcement*, he explains how a person could become so invested in their work that other aspects of their life suffered, eventually causing their work to suffer. Clearly, being a workaholic does not make you a better supervisor.

Over the years, I have become a proponent of scheduling hobbies into our busy lives to help balance life and become a better person. I know that supervisors overly invested in their job can experience boredom when they are away from the job. Boredom can lead to poor health and lifestyle choices including, but certainly not limited to, overeating, smoking, and drug or alcohol abuse. Leisure activities have been shown to serve as a counterbalance to many of those harmful lifestyle choices. In addition to reducing stress, leisure activities have been shown to provide positive physiological changes including a reduced heart rate and reduced blood pressure.

According to a study published in the *Annals of Behavioral Medicine*, the positive results from leisure activities are typically experienced not only during the activity, but even hours after the activity. While few could argue the benefits of being physically active, a Mayo Clinic study found that those middle-aged adults who engaged in a creative hobby (something that required cognitive skills) experienced a reduced risk of memory loss or dementia as they aged. This was supported by a study published in *The International Journal of Alzheimer's Disease* that reported that playing a musical instrument during adulthood is significantly associated with reduced risk of cognitive impairment and dementia. Clearly, leisure activities have physical and psychological health benefits, but how do we find the time?

Dr. Gilmartin says it is about time management. If you understand the importance of good health, you will understand it is worth whatever time it takes to achieve a balanced lifestyle. Larry Winget in his book, *Shut Up, Stop Whining, and Get a Life,* says it is not so much about time management as it is about priorities. Make your hobby a priority. Here are some additional thoughts on leisure activities and setting priorities:

- Hobbies are something you actively do on a regular basis. Interests are something you watch others do, or do yourself once or twice a year. Have lots of interests, but get at least one hobby. Watching WWII stories on the History Channel is an interest. Learning how to play a new musical instrument is a hobby.

- Do not wait for retirement. Do not spend your career thinking about the hobbies you will start when you retire. Just because they give you a fishing pole at your retirement does not mean you will like fishing.

- Hobbies should have a learning curve. Learning to play tennis or play the guitar requires a skill. A single parachute jump while you are strapped to an instructor as you celebrate your birthday may check something off your bucket list, but it is not a hobby.

- Hobbies with learning curves are sometimes frustrating or embarrassing in the beginning, but the benefits are still there. As your skill develops, the enjoyment and benefits will increase.

- There are jerks in hobbies, too. Some of the same personalities you dislike at work exist in a hobby. Do not let your new hobby become more stressful than work.

TIP: Hobbies, in which you regularly participate, can help you achieve a more balanced life, while at the same time helping you become a better family member at home and a better supervisor at work.

Tip #28

Sarcasm

We often think our sarcasm is funny. We sometimes use it to get subordinates to do what we want without needing to be confrontational. Some employees understand the use of sarcasm for that purpose and understand the point the supervisor is trying to make. Other employees, nonetheless, might become angry at what they perceive is a demeaning comment. Still other employees miss the point entirely, because they do not understand a message is being communicated through the passive use of humor. Those differences in possible responses make my point. The problem with supervisors using sarcasm is that we really never know how our message will be received.

If you use sarcasm frequently as part of your communication style and think it is well received by your subordinates because no one has ever complained, do not be too quick to think your sarcasm is working. Some people do not complain, because you are the boss. At least, they do not complain to you or to your face. Clearly, there are more effective (and less risky) ways to get employees to do what we want, rather than using sarcasm.

Obviously, supervisors are not the only ones who make sarcastic comments. You probably have an employee or two who use sarcasm against you. I call them snipers, because they seem to enjoy taking shots at us from behind cover. They use humor as camouflage for their indirect criticism and passive-aggressive attacks. You cannot afford to be seen as tolerating sarcastic comments which undermine their authority. Humor is a great stress reliever and does build camaraderie, but it should not be used as a weapon against you. Never let the sniper, taking his shot at you, get away with a demeaning, derogatory, and sarcastic comment. It is not funny - it is called unacceptable behavior.

When you catch the sniper in the act and call him on his behavior, he will generally try to brush it off as simply humor (that is the camouflage he hopes to hide behind). Probably 99% of the backstabbing, passive-aggressive, sniper-type employees are going to say, "Oh, I did not mean anything by it. I was just kidding." You do not need to do anything else at that point. You have just put the sniper on notice that you are aware of his tactics. You recognized him and brought him out in the daylight. You have taken off his camouflage. It lets him know, without being confrontational, that you will not tolerate disrespectful or demeaning comments. In that rare instance where he says, "Yea, that was a shot – so what?" At least you know where you stand, and it is probably time for a one-on-one discussion in private with that disrespectful employee.

Here are a few suggestions for dealing with the sarcastic employee:

- Sarcasm is not a contest. Do not try to one-up a sarcastic employee by responding with an even more sarcastic comment.

- Keep your emotions in check. That includes both comments and body language. Laughing or getting angry encourages more sarcasm.

- If the goal of the sarcasm was to get an emotional rise out of you and you did not take the bait, the sarcastic employee may ask, "Did you get it?" Your matter-of-fact response should be, "Yes, I got it." No need to add anything else. Your short matter-of-fact response will send a clear message.

- If a sarcastic comment is made to you that you find demeaning, confront the employee using an assertive (not aggressive) communication style. Say something like, "That sounded sarcastic. That sounded like a shot. Was that how you meant it?"

TIP: Sarcasm is a passive-aggressive form of communication that seldom sends a clear or positive message. It should not be used by us, nor tolerated when used against us.

Tip #29

Chronic Complainers

Chronic complainers do what they do without needing a triggering event to set them off. It is a long-term behavioral trait and one you are not likely to cure. Remember you cannot fix people, and you are not likely to alter personalities. Even if you did give the chronic complainer a valid solution to his problem, it would not likely make a dent in his complaining because he was not really looking for a solution. Chronic complainers are looking for someone with whom to commiserate - someone who will listen to their complaints, however, unfounded - and maybe even agree with them. And they keep complaining, because it works. We keep listening, keep providing solutions they do not want to hear and, by our actions or inactions, we keep encouraging them to continue complaining.

Do not confuse chronic complainers with an employee that comes to you occasionally with a legitimate complaint. It is a supervisor's job to listen to their employees' suggestions, concerns, issues, or problems. Sometimes we can offer solutions. Sometimes we can help them find their own solutions. Sometimes those good employees, who may be situational-complainers, just need the sympathetic ear of a caring supervisor to listen.

Chronic complainers are a different breed. Your task in dealing with them is to find a way to get them to stop wasting your time and get them back to work. Here are some strategies that might help:

- **Venting allowed (sparingly).** If a person rarely complains and they are upset about an issue, it is usually good to listen. Venting may allow the problem to fix itself.

- **Do not argue.** It is a waste of time to argue with a chronic complainer or to try to convince them their complaint is unjustified.

- **Empathy and redirection.** If they are complaining about people or equipment, you can show empathy and let them know that you understand how frustrating, annoying, or aggravating a situation might be, and then redirect them to the task at hand.

- **Chronic optimism.** They are complaining to you because they want to commiserate with you. The last thing they want to hear is optimism or that you like the person they are complaining about. That is good news for you. It will not fix the problem (if there is a problem), but it may cause them to go find someone else to commiserate with.

- **Be direct.** Sometimes you have to be direct and tell them you do not have time to meet at that moment. Instruct them to come back at a time that is convenient for you.

- **Ask them to put it in writing.** Most chronic complainers do not want to put their complaints in writing. Some do not even want their names used. If they do not want to be part of the solution, they should not be wasting your time.

- **Ask for a solution.** Ask them how they would solve the problem. If they have a good idea, use it.

- **Switch to problem solving.** Anytime you can include them in a solution, there is a chance you may correct a legitimate problem. As a bonus, if the solution involves more work for the chronic complainer, he is less likely to come back.

TIP: Chronic complainers are not looking for solutions. Do not encourage their behavior, argue, or confront them. And do not squander your valuable time listening to repeated baseless complaints. Deal with the chronic complainer assertively and, whenever possible, include them in the solution.

Tip #30

Real Engagement

Managing by Walking Around (MBWA) is a strategy that works, but it requires more than merely walking around. For MBWA to be successful, it requires engagement with employees.

A municipal clerical worker had "survived" five supervisors over her long municipal career. A new administrator was hired from within the organization. The employees generally felt that since she had no previous supervisory experience, her tenure would be as bad and as short as her predecessors. Obviously, a negative work environment had existed there for some time.

One morning, the new administrator came into the municipal clerical employee's office. The clerical employee said the administrator was carrying a clipboard, which initially made her think she was in trouble. Instinctively, the clerical worker asked, "What did I do?" The administrator, not understanding the question, said, "What do you mean?" After a brief pause, the administrator sat down and said, "I just wanted to meet with you if you had a few moments, and ask you how things were going." The clerical worker was stunned and did not know what to say.

Finally after an awkward pause she said, "I have worked here for 19 years, and I never had a boss really ask me how things were going." She went on to explain that sometimes a boss would see her in the hall and in passing ask, "How are things going?" as he continued walking. She said that she knew they were busy and thought it was just a courteous automatic response. She said no other conversation ever took place in those brief encounters.

The new administrator responded that she was not busy at that moment and had specifically made time in her schedule to meet with the clerical employee. The clerical employee said later that the new administrator had done more to build morale, trust, and commitment in those few minutes than all of the other administrators had, combined over the many years she had worked for them.

Here are a few suggestions that can make a difference in your MBWA efforts:

- **Automatic salutations are not a connection.** A salutation as you pass in the hall may be courteous, but if there is never more conversation, it feels like an automatic response without substance.

- **Salutations beat no salutations.** Courteous comments in passing when you are actually busy are better than ignoring the employee.

- **Schedule time.** Maybe most of the time your MBWA is relegated to passing comments or observations because you are a busy supervisor. If so, schedule a time when you can meet with individual employees and ask them about their issues and concerns.

- **Focus.** During those one-on-one encounters, hold off on all phone calls or interruptions. It should be about you and that employee. What is working? What is not working? What can we do differently to help you do your job? If you appear busy, the employee's responses will be painfully short and the meeting will not serve its purpose.

- **Take notes.** Take a pad of paper and write down the employee's suggestions and concerns. Writing down comments made by the employee says you actually care about what is being said and want to review the information in more detail at a later time. In fact, the very act of bringing in a notepad signifies you believe employee feedback is important and you want to record it accurately (and subsequently be able to give credit for good ideas).

TIP. Engagement with employees is more than courteous salutations as you pass in the hall. Engagement and effective MBWA requires you take the time to really hear your employees.

Tip #31

Predictability

He was a police officer in a 150-man metropolitan police department. His early work record in the department was marked by disciplinary issues. Over the course of several years, he appeared before the disciplinary board of the department for repeated behavioral issues, including conduct unbecoming an officer. Sometimes the charges would be dismissed, and sometimes he would be disciplined, but was never fired.

One night he was assigned to an executive protection detail at a theater. He showed up three hours late for the assignment. When he finally arrived, he was unhappy with his assigned post, because it did not allow him to watch the performance. He left his post to find a better seat. At intermission, he left the theater entirely to go to a bar across the street for a few drinks.

The date was April 14, 1865. The place was Ford's Theater in Washington DC. The person he was assigned to protect was President Abraham Lincoln. The officer with the history of repeated discipline problems was Frank Parker. He followed a behavioral pattern that had become typical for him and apparently acceptable to his supervisors. As a result of his absence from his post that night, John Wilkes Booth gained easy access to President Abraham Lincoln and killed him with a single gunshot.

Parker was never disciplined for his dereliction of duty that night. He remained on the police force until 1868, when he was finally fired for sleeping on duty. Apparently, he never changed his work habits. It took one final act of sleeping on duty before someone in his department finally realized his repeated behavior justified termination.

Just as they did in 1865, patterns of unacceptable behavior can predict future behavior. To say that the past always predicts future behavior would be an oversimplification. A single isolated incident does not always predict that the incident will be repeated. People make mistakes and are often willing to learn from those mistakes. But a repeated pattern of behavior is worth taking a close look at. Consider the following:

- **Patterns**. A pattern of similar unacceptable behavior is likely to predict future behavior, if similar circumstances exist and the individual has made no effort to change, and/or there has been no effective intervention by supervisory personnel.

- **Habitual.** High-frequency, habitual behaviors are more predictive than infrequent behaviors.

- **Change.** People can and do change, but not often, and then only when THEY want to change. If the person engaging in unacceptable behavior makes no effort to change, plan on past behavior predicting future behavior.

- **Corrective Feedback.** The absence of corrective feedback is likely to allow, if not actually encourage, the pattern of unacceptable behavior to be repeated, making it more likely that past bad behavior will predict future bad behavior.

- **Minor becomes major.** Officer Parker's repeated minor incidents led him to believe that such behavior was normal. His behavior apparently seemed normal to his department's disciplinary board as well. Even his behavior on April 14, 1865, could have been expected. Being late for work, sleeping on duty, drinking on duty, or being absent from his post probably seemed unimportant to Parker at the time, but the results were catastrophic.

TIP: A pattern of similar unacceptable behaviors repeated over a relatively short time span can serve as a predictor of future behavior. The desire of a person to change, combined with corrective feedback from supervisors (or discipline when appropriate), seems to be the only factors that may alter that prediction.

Tip #32

Rule Benders

I had just finished speaking at the 2015 International Association of Chiefs of Police annual conference and was flying home on Southwest Airlines. I had position number A23. There was a beer-drinking guy in front of me. A man approached the beer drinker and said, "I'm A20. What number are you?" The beer drinker said, "I'm A25, but it really doesn't matter." I was thinking that if it really doesn't matter, "Why don't you take your A25 boarding pass and go back behind me where you belong?" But I remained silent. A few minutes later a lady with a boarding pass clearly marked B25 tried to get in line in the A section. She did not understand the boarding process, but was immediately rebuffed by numerous other people in the A section. The beer-drinking, position-jumper was tolerated as a rule bender. But the section-jumping woman was seen as a rule breaker and that could not be allowed by the others in line. It seemed to me that it was the same offense, just different in degrees. We seem much more comfortable confronting rule breakers than rule benders.

The beer-drinking, position-jumper is like a lot of employees who believe that rules are not hard and fast, but more like guidelines that can be ignored at their whim - just as long as you do not carry the rule breaking too far. It reminds me of the employee who is frequently late for work - but just a little late. The tardy employee may think being a little late is rule bending and not that big a deal. But it is a big deal to those employees who follow the rules and do their job, only to hear chronic rule benders say it does not matter. What is even more demotivating for the average employee is when they observe chronic rule benders who are seldom confronted by their supervisors.

Do the little things matter when it comes to inappropriate behavior? They should. They certainly matter to the other employees who are watching and hoping for a supervisor willing to address the problem. Consider the following:

- **What are the rules?** Know what the rules are because your rule benders do. Rules can be written policies or your orders or instructions. If a behavior bothers you, make sure the employee knows your expectations. You do not need to write a policy in every case, but employees need to know the rules you expect them to live by.

- **Why does the rule exist?** Rules, policies, or your instructions should have a purpose and reason for their existence, and that reason should never be vindictiveness. If it is a bad rule, change it. If it is a stupid rule, get rid of it. You are not always required to explain the reason for a rule, but you should be able to, if needed.

- **Is the culture contrary to the rule?** If you have rules that are habitually ignored, you should either get rid of the rule to match the culture or change the culture. Do not have rules that conflict with common practices.

- **Should I be flexible?** Your flexibility should come into play with your consequences and not with a valid, reasonable rule. A first-time offender who is ten minutes late might simply be required to give you an explanation. An employee who is two hours late might require counseling. A chronically tardy employee might require formal progressive discipline. Flexibility in consequences is much easier on you than trying to determine how many minutes late really constitutes a rule violation.

TIP: Rule Benders and Rule Breakers are the same. The degree of seriousness in the violation of a rule or your instructions may require flexibility in the consequences, but should not negate the fact that a valid, reasonable, and known rule or instruction was violated or ignored.

Tip #33

Attention to Details

When I travel for business, I sometimes find myself forced to eat at "fast food" restaurants. On more than a few occasions, I have received my reasonably priced food in a reasonable period of time only to carry my tray to a dirty table in a dirty dining area. The poor impression that leaves is compounded if, when I use the restroom, that, too, appears unclean. I might cut the restaurant some slack if their problems were the result of being extremely busy. However, there have been times when I made this observation, a restaurant was virtually empty.

Some would argue it is an employee issue - a lack of their self-initiative and lack of work ethic by low paid employees. I think it is more likely a supervision problem. Granted, I know nothing about the fast food business. What I do know is that more than once I have considered boycotting a particular chain entirely because I blame the entire chain for the problems caused by a few employees or their supervisor's lack of attention to detail.

I could blame their corporate office since they set policy and priorities, but since implementation occurs at the manager's level, I think the blame rests with individual supervisors. Let's face it, it would be great if all employees had an outstanding work ethic, but that is probably an unrealistic expectation. And since policies and job descriptions cannot possibly cover every conceivable circumstance, something more is needed. That something is a supervisor's clearly stated expectation.

If the shift manager told every employee that one of his expectations was cleanliness in the dining area and restrooms and that it was a priority above everything else when they are not waiting customers, I think the culture in those fast food restaurants might begin to change. Communicating a supervisor's expectations and priorities about the small, but important, details of the job is what being a supervisor is all about - getting employees to do their job better. This failure to meet or even know a supervisor's expectations is a problem not unique to the fast food industry. It applies to all occupations.

Here are a few suggestions on communicating your expectations.

- **They are not you.** Your employees are not you and some will not have your work ethic or self-initiative. Some need more direction than others. Do not assume that they know what is expected.

- **Clarify Roles.** Typically, job descriptions only cover 50-75% of what employees might be called to do. Policies frequently tell people what not to do.

Supervisors must set the parameters for the role each employee is expected to play.

- **Set Expectations.** Each supervisor may have his own expectations and priorities. If not informed of those expectations, employees operate based on the best information they have. That information may be from a supervisor with completely different expectations than yours. Set your own expectations for your employees.

- **Do not micromanage.** Setting expectations is not micromanagement. Set expectations and then provide support and guidance.

- **Build Trust.** The higher the level of trust between you and your subordinates, the easier the communications will be and the more likely they will be to meet or exceed your expectations.

TIP: If you want your employees to pay attention to details, do not assume they automatically know your expectations. Expectations and priorities should be set by individual supervisors through regular proactive communication efforts and continual feedback.

Tip #34

Space Cadets

Have you ever worked with an employee who at times seems a little clueless? Maybe he daydreams when the nature of his work requires concentration and attention to details. Such employees sometimes respond to your questions with a seemingly unrelated comment that makes you think maybe they did not hear the question. People often refer to these employees as *space cadets*. If you have one, and you are wondering how in God's name your organization ever hired the guy in the first place, the answer is simple. They are generally friendly people. They are not overly aggressive or power hungry. At the employment interview, he did not appear that he would become a chronic complainer or discipline problem. And sometimes all you were looking for was a new employee who would not cause any problems.

Employees who fit this description are not stupid and are not bad employees. They often are abstract thinkers who concern themselves more with ideas and possibilities, rather than on facts or the logical steps required to follow through on their ideas. They do not think in a linear, step-by-step process. When they are talking about potential results that will happen at point D, they sometimes forget they have to complete points A, B, and C first. And if they do see that all those steps are required, they may not be good at communicating that understanding. Details are important. And sometimes this employee misses the details. They are not good at mundane tasks. But unfortunately, most jobs occasionally require mundane tasks.

As a supervisor for this employee, you can help them become a better employee while making your life a little easier at the same time by doing the following:

- **Ask for details in their ideas.** They appreciate supervisors who listen to their ideas and insights. They may have good ideas, but lack the details of how to bring that idea to fruition.

- **Attention to tasks.** People who do not enjoy doing mundane, but necessary, tasks often find a way to avoid or delay the task. While no one likes micromanagement, this employee may need some additional supervision.

- **Follow Through.** These employees may be enthusiastic at the start of an assignment, but get easily bored with the details and fail to follow through. Supervisors should not take it for granted that the necessary follow-though will be completed.

- **Set expectations.** Clearly define your expectations and reinforce as necessary. Do not delegate without specific interim feedback points.

- **Step-by-Step Tasks.** These employees may be more effective at completing tasks when the supervisor breaks a large assignment into a series of smaller steps. When the step is completed, the next step is assigned.

- **Supervise.** These employees need to be supervised. They do not need to be micromanaged, but they do need a supervisor who pays attention.

- **Worth listening to.** They have a different way of thinking than step-by-step lineal thinkers. They often have good ideas whose benefits are not immediately apparent. Their long-range concerns often prove true and should not be dismissed.

TIPS: Even space cadets can become valuable team members. Use their strengths (i.e. abstract thought and future planning to handle ongoing issues), while realizing that they need supervision and feedback to help them complete some of the more mundane tasks required of the job.

Tip #35

Sincerity

Late in my career, I finally realized that my job was not simply to complete tasks, but to get my employees to do their jobs better. I came to realize that one of the many ways to do that is to build trust. I also came to understand that one of the many ways to build trust is to show you care and that one of the many ways to show you care is to have causal conversations about things important to your employees.

    The difficulty in my transition from task-oriented leader to someone who thinks casual conversations are important was that the transition felt uncomfortable. It is not that we task-oriented leaders are incapable of people skills, it is just that (at the beginning at least) it sometimes feels uncomfortable and a little forced. It might even feel like you are faking it.

    The good news is that if you keep at these trust-building efforts, it will become easier. In fact, it will become a habit for you and an accepted and expected routine for your employees. This is clearly a long-term strategy for performance improvement, and not a quick-fix technique.

Most supervisors find any change they make in themselves at first uncomfortable and forced, and then easier, and then more routine, and finally, an important part of their daily activities. This transition takes time. One supervisor told me his boss had tried the transition from task-oriented to people-focused and failed miserably. He said the boss came across as being uncomfortable and insincere. In fact, he said he thought that apparent insincerity caused more problems than if the boss never engaged with his employees. The problem was compounded by the fact that the boss only made the effort for a couple of days before giving up and reverting to his old task-oriented ways.

Any change you make in your work habits may at first be uncomfortable to both you and your employees. But there is a difference between being uncomfortable and insincere. An insincere supervisor is taking action to manipulate the employee in hopes of a quick fix. Conversely, the sincere supervisor wants to do what is right, even though he may at first feel uncomfortable in doing so. And the sincere supervisor keeps at it until his engagement efforts become the new normal.

Employees will also believe you are insincere if your warm and causal five-minute morning conversation is incongruent with the way you treat them the remainder of the day. The boss who is overly friendly one minute and a jerk the rest of the day is seldom seen as sincere. Showing you care is not always easy. Showing you are sincere about caring is sometimes even harder.

Here are a few ideas to help confirm your sincerity:

- **Be consistent.** Do not be one kind of caring supervisor during your scheduled casual daily conversation, and an uncaring taskmaster or workaholic the rest of the day, who never bothers to look for additional opportunities to engage.

- **Find opportunities.** Do not make your scheduled daily time for employee engagement the only time you have casual conversations. Look for opportunities to engage throughout the day.

- **Be tenacious.** Do not quit trying just because you do not see a miracle cure for problem employees. It is too easy to fall back into the task-oriented trap when you realize things are not changing as fast as you would like. Keep at it. It is called work for a reason.

TIP: Do it for the right reasons. Causal conversations with employees may build trust and improve morale, communications, and commitment, but those are side benefits. The reason you engage with your employees is because you care about those you supervise. And having conversations about things that are important to them is one way to show you care.

Tip #36

Fault Finders

Have you ever worked with an employee, a subordinate, peer, or even a boss, who seemed to find fault with everyone and everything? The *Fault Finder* might be a hard worker, but you probably would not call him a good worker because that would imply that he was able to do the required tasks without alienating his coworkers or causing you problems. He tolerates you, but complains about almost all of his coworkers and other supervisors.

Too often, *Fault Finders* want to share their negative beliefs with coworkers. You may hear grumbling from several employees, but the source is often a *Fault Finder* who complained to everyone who would listen. When employees talk about having heard something that "everyone" is complaining about, ask for details and for the source of the complaint. You may find that some of the people complaining do not have an issue themselves, but are reporting what was initiated by the *Fault Finder*. It is amazing how one *Fault Finder* can make enough noise to make it appear that the entire organization is unhappy, when, in reality, the problems rests with a single person.

Fault Finders think it is their job to point out problems you have overlooked. In their continuing effort to do so, the *Fault Finder* is more of a problem-creator than problem-finder. Once the *Fault Finder* has cemented his reputation (which does not take long) as a complainer, others tend to use him for their own purposes. Sometimes people with even minor issues will bring them to the *Fault Finder* just so he can stir the pot while the instigator sits back and smiles in obscurity at the storm he created. People with their own personal problems and complaints often look for someone like the *Fault Finder* to dump their issues on because of his appetite for misinformation.

If you have a *fault finder* working for you, there are some ways to minimize his or her damage.

- **Positives cancel out negatives.** You can often achieve good results by countering a negative with a positive. If he complains about a coworker, point out a positive about that person that you typically observe. *Fault Finders* are looking for people who feel the same way they do, so they can commiserate. They will not stick around long complaining to you if your responses are positive.

- **Believe In Others.** Whenever he complains to you about the motives of a coworker, express your belief in that person unless that person has proven himself to you personally to not deserve such support. Even then, do not share that doubt with the *Fault Finder*.

- **Encourage Resolution.** If he complains about another coworker, suggest he talk to that person to resolve the issue. His problem is not automatically your problem. It is often best for them to meet one-on-one. If he keeps coming back to you with the same issue about the same person but has refused to meet with him, stop the discussion. Do not take on a problem that is clearly his responsibility.

- **Come With A Solution.** We can often help our employees find a solution to a problem, but he is not necessarily looking for a solution. While it should not be a requirement that everyone that comes to you with a problem has a solution, it might be worth considering making that a rule for your *Fault Finders*. You may find it beneficial if they, at least, put some thought into a solution and how that solution might be implemented.

TIP: ***Fault Finders*** **have a talent for spreading their negativity throughout an organization like a spark igniting numerous small brushfires. The best way to extinguish a fire is at its source. Deal directly with your *Fault Finders* before the fire spreads.**

Tip #37

The Blame Game

Fear of making mistakes stifles creativity. We want our employees to be creative, to find better, more effective and efficient ways to do their job. But too often today, employees are not only afraid to make mistakes, many use *The Blame Game* as a defensive measure when something goes wrong.

    Blaming is contagious and, if left unaddressed, can create a culture of blaming within your organization with harmful results for both employee morale and performance. You know a culture of blame exists if you observe a general lack of accountability or a failure to understand specific job responsibilities by your employees. That combined with a hesitancy to admit mistakes or attempts to cover up those mistakes, rather than fixing them, are good indicators that a culture of blame exists.

    Recognizing when *The Blame Game* is being played is extremely important. Whenever you find employees trying to deflect attention from the real issue by blaming others for the problem, or whenever an employee brings up similar behaviors other employees may have engaged in without correction in the past, rather than accepting responsibility, *The Blame Game* is being played on you.

The Blame Game must be stopped at the top. All supervisors must be willing to accept responsibility for their actions, omissions, behaviors, and mistakes. They must stop blaming their supervisors, the boss, the lack of funding, poor pay, the equipment, entitled employees, or the public for their own bad decisions or bad behavior. Supervisors must set the example by not blaming others when the responsibility for an issue rests in their hands. This includes not shifting blame on their boss when told to instruct subordinates on an undesirable task. Too often supervisors shift blame for an order in an effort to avoid responsibility in giving the assignment. Do not blame others for orders you are instructed to give to your subordinates.

When *The Blame Game* is played on you by a subordinate, consider these suggestions:

- **Be Clear.** Make sure the employee has a clear understanding of his responsibilities and your expectations.

- **Sometimes it is the supervisor's fault.** Accept it and be the first to admit mistakes and take responsibility for your employees when it is appropriate. Sometimes it is not the supervisor's fault, but the supervisor is still responsible and should accept that responsibility.

- **Stop it when you see it.** If a conversation with your subordinate changes to blame-shifting, refocus the topic back to the issue. It is about correcting the mistake and preventing it from happening again, not about assigning blame or making excuses. Refocus back to the issue at hand and your expectations for future behavior.

- **Blame is not the same as corrective feedback.** There are times when subordinates make mistakes. Corrective feedback to prevent the problem from reoccurring is not blaming.

- **Focus on learning.** Create a culture of learning, and not a culture of blame. Let employees know it is OK to make mistakes. Making mistakes and learning from those mistakes - rather than learning how to avoid or hide mistakes - should be the goal if you want your organization to keep moving forward.

TIP: Stop *The Blame Game* in its tracks by refocusing on the issue at hand, the person's responsibilities, and your expectations for the future.

Tip #38

What We Control

Sometimes we lose good leaders to transfers, other jobs, or retirement. It can be disheartening for employees if they felt a connection to that leader. In some cases, that leader was your inspiration when you first joined the organization. If a lot of those inspiring people move on and are not replaced by other good people, it becomes increasingly harder to stay motivated and committed to the organization. This circumstance can exist in any organization, including those where you volunteer your time in hopes of reducing stress.

    I experienced this dilemma first hand when I realized my interest and self-motivation in the fife and drum organization I had belonged to for ten years started to diminish after the departure of an inspiring leader. The organization plays 18th and 19th century fife and drum music, and to maintain a desired level of proficiency, members practice regularly at home and at weekly group practice sessions. I had missed numerous weekly practices because of business and had missed a few more because of the long drive, bad weather, and a host of other excuses I made up for myself. I knew I needed to get myself out of demotivation mode and either get back into the activity, or leave for good and spend my time doing other activities.

I decided to try to motivate myself and start going to practices again. I made the three-hour drive in the rain at night and arrived early. Our leader (whose predecessor had inspired my real commitment) arrived 45 minutes late. Upon arrival, she mumbled something that sounded like, "Sorry for being late." Sorry does not really feel like sorry if you have said it many times before. Those thoughts must have shown on my face because the next words she spoke directly to me - were, "I've had a really shitty week."

As my frustration over several years of bad leadership rose, and my personal motivation sank, I was feeling more than a little disgruntled. After a long absence from weekly practices, I had come that day in hopes of getting inspired and motivated. I was thinking that was a mistake, because I now felt less motivated than before. And then I realized one important fact. I have no control over our group's leader. I am not her boss and have no control over how she treats others. I have no control over whether she shows up on time. I have no control over the bad leadership of those I do not supervise, or the bad examples they set. I do not even have any control over the fact that this leader seems to thrive on negativity and sarcasm. I control only one thing, and that one thing is me. I control only how I feel and how I react to circumstances and people (including this leader).

On the drive home, I had plenty of time to think. Do I want to quit this group because some of the really good leaders and co-members that I liked have moved on? Do I want to quit the group because the current leader is a morale killer? The answer came to me by asking one more question. Why did I join the group in the first place? I did not join because of the leader (as good as he was), who was there when I first started. I did not even know him before I started. I did not join because I thought I was going to like all of the people in the group. I did not know any of the people when I first started. I joined because I liked the particular activity. I joined because I thought I would get personal satisfaction from belonging to the group and participating in the group's activities.

I had to reevaluate what I can control and what I cannot control. Here are some thoughts on the issue that apply to both our full time jobs and leisure activities:

1. We first took the job, joined the group, or engaged in the activity because we thought it would be enjoyable - not every day maybe, but at least more times than not. If you really hate your job or hate the activity every day (regardless of how much you get paid), move on and stop making everyone else miserable. Life is too short to hate what you do every day.

2. We thought the job or activity would be personally satisfying and rewarding. It would make us a better person. We would feel needed, valued, and make a difference in the lives of others. In some cases we

identify closely with the job or activity or the people in our group - it is who we are, and proud of it. If that is not the case, maybe it is time to consider moving on.

3. There are no guarantees that you are going to like all your coworkers, subordinates, or supervisors. They are not your family, and there is no requirement to be best friends with anyone. If you do like a few of them, consider it a bonus. If you do not like them, look at Points #1 and #2.

4. There are no guarantees that the people who lead you will be always be good leaders, treat you fairly, or inspire and motivate you. If they do, consider yourself very fortunate, because not everyone works for such a leader. If they do not, look at Points #1 and #2.

TIP: We cannot control those who lead us. We can only control our feelings and our reactions to those individuals or circumstances. Keep in mind why you took the job or joined the group in the first place, and keep yourself motivated for those same reasons.

Tip #39

Coaching

You want your employees to do the job for which they were hired. If they exceed expectations and do a great job, that would be terrific. If they could do a great job without causing you any headaches - even better. Sadly, that great performance on their part - without any effort on your part - is not likely to occur, at least not with most employees. Most employees are going to need a little guidance. Some, in fact, are going to need a lot of guidance. And unfortunately, some will refuse your guidance and may need discipline.

When performance is poor, too often we think the only solution is progressive discipline. Examples of progressive discipline might include verbal and written warnings, suspension, and even termination. Some supervisors even use formal discipline (or the threat of formal discipline) as their primary tool to get the performance they want from their employees. Usually the results are disappointing. While some employees may deserve a disciplinary response, others might benefit more from coaching.

Coaching differs from counseling. Counseling is often formalized and part of the disciplinary process. Coaching, on the one hand, is a formal conversation without the automatic progressive discipline connotation. Coaching can be used to give the employee advice and guidance. Regular coaching will often result in greater employee confidence and competence.

To make sure coaching does not feel like discipline, it should be done on a regular basis, and not just in response to employee errors or poor performance. Counseling and discipline typically occur when something is wrong. Coaching is more like a regular scheduled conversation about how the employee is doing on the job.

Listed below are some guidelines for coaching sessions:

- **Schedule.** Schedule a 10-minute coaching session on your calendar, just like you would for any other appointment. Make sure the employee knows the date and time in advance, to minimize his stress.

- **Frequency.** Some supervisors do these sessions once a month. The time period is not as important as the fact that it is on a regular basis.

- **Content.** The content should be guidance for improvement. If you are in the enviable position of having an employee who needs no improvement, spend the time talking about the good job he is doing, his career goals, or what he thinks you could do to make him more effective.

- **Document.** Use your department's performance management software, if you have one; an email to the employee recapping the session; or your own *supervisor's notebook*. If your organization does performance evaluations, this documentation can be used to support why you rated an employee at a particular level.

- **If it is new.** If you have never done this with employees before, it may be scary for them at first. They will think they have done something wrong. It may take several monthly coaching sessions before they understand your positive intent. Building trust and improving performance takes time!

- **Do not wait.** Do not wait for a problem to arise before scheduling, and do not confuse coaching with either training or disciplinary action. Coaching, counseling, training, and discipline each have a purpose. Coaching is just one of your tools.

TIP: Progressive discipline is a useful tool, but it is not the right tool in every case. Coaching provides the employee with the guidance needed to improve, and provides you and those who supervise you with documentation that you took steps to help the employee meet or exceed expectations.

Tip #40

Sick Leave Abuse

We spend a lot of our time worrying about why employees are absent. It is probably the wrong issue to worry about. Yes, it matters if an employee calls in sick and then goes to a Super Bowl party. Yes, it matters if an employee calls in sick and starts out a day early on his vacation. Certainly flagrant inappropriate use of sick time must be addressed. But in most cases, we do not know for sure if the employee is really sick, took a day off to take his elderly mother to a doctor's appointment, or stayed home because he felt like he needed a mental health day. If we focus our efforts only on making sure employees have good excuses for calling in sick, all we do is train them to come up with better excuses.

In his book, *Discipline Without Punishment*, Dick Grote recommends we focus instead on things we know for sure. While we may never know for sure why an employee is absent, we do know he is absent and we would like him to be absent less often. It is called "Regular Attendance" according to Grote, and it is one of the most basic requirements of any job. If sick time usage becomes excessive, Grote recommends counseling employees by explaining the attendance policy of your organization and your expectations to the employee.

I agree with Grote's suggestion that it is not too much to expect that our employees show up to work, fully prepared, on time, every day, for the entire duration of the work day. Unless they meet a very narrow set of circumstances, any variation of that is a failure to meet expectations and a violation of policy. It is really all about expectations and holding employees accountable to those expectations.

Some policies or collective bargaining agreements require doctor's notes after a certain number of sick days or "events." These requirements are sometimes successful in reducing the number of days used, but they seldom change the entitlement attitude of employees who feel their sick days are the equivalent of additional vacation days. While obtaining a doctor's note may be an inconvenience, it is certainly not difficult. What is needed more than having new policies is supervisors willing to help change the sick-time-entitlement mindset.

The following guidelines are not meant to be a cure-all for sick time abuse, but rather should serve as some guidelines for reducing such abuse:

- **Flagrant Violations.** If an employee is observed drinking at a bar after he calls in sick, he is abusing sick time. To ignore these violations encourages the behavior to be repeated. Ignoring the situation also demotivates employees who never take fake sick days. Do not ignore it even if you are feeling guilty about the mental health days you took earlier in your career. No one ever said being a supervisor was going to be easy. Counseling or discipline is warranted.

- **Abuse Patterns.** Abuse patterns violate the organization's attendance expectations even when they are not a flagrant violation of policy. Look for patterns which may include last day before vacation or first day back, first or last day of shift rotation, repeated weekends, or any other repeating occurrence of sick time usage. Counseling is appropriate in most of these cases.

- **Above Average Usage.** Consider determining the average sick time use in your organization. Then make a determination on what constitutes excessive. For example, 25% above average might be considered excessive. Employees who use more sick time than that predetermined number would be counseled on both policy and your expectations. Counseling is appropriate in most of these cases.

- **Work Patterns.** Going home sick from work (without any apparent illness) after being given an assignment they do not like or after having a disagreement with a supervisor is sick time abuse.

Counseling and or discipline is appropriate in most of these cases.

- **Improvement.** It is not enough for an employee in counseling to say they will "try to improve." Taking only 14 sick days this year when you took 15 last year is not an improvement. If you are counseling this employee, you want correction and commitment and not just improvement.

TIP: Regular attendance means showing up for work every scheduled day and working the entire shift. It is the most basic of job expectations. Counsel those who regularly fail to meet that expectation, even if there is no apparent flagrant policy violation.

Tip #41

No Surprises Please

In the winter of 1979, I was coming to the end of a two-year tour aboard the U.S. Coast Guard Cutter *Eagle*. I was a Damage Controlman, and had no real immediate supervisor to tell me what was expected of me, or how I was doing. In theory I worked for an Engineering Officer, whom I almost never saw except at quarters every morning when the ship's officers took attendance. When you almost never see your boss, you tend to assume you must be doing OK.

The *Eagle* spent that winter in a shipyard in Baltimore for a major overhaul. Engineering Division supervisors, like me, were requested to submit a worklist to the Engineering Officer for his approval. I submitted my list, and received no feedback, so I proceeded working through the list as part of my daily routine. About a month later, I received a call from Coast Guard headquarters that I was being transferred, and they were not refilling my position. I was pleased, as several of my friends had already been transferred. The Engineering Officer was not pleased. He said I wasn't going anywhere, because he did not want to lose the position. The Captain finally intervened, saying if I had orders to be transferred, then I was being transferred.

Nevertheless, the Engineering Officer got the last word. He got to do my performance evaluation on the day I was transferred. Those were the lowest marks I received during my entire Coast Guard career. I was livid and embarrassed. When I tried to ask why I got such low marks, the Engineering Officer said I had spent too much time worrying about being transferred and had submitted an insufficient worklist at the start of the yard period.

To say that a surprisingly low performance evaluation can make someone angry would be an understatement. If over the course of an evaluation period you seldom hear from a supervisor, you assume you are at least meeting the minimum acceptable performance standard. Fortunately, the evaluation marks at my next duty station were excellent. I was grateful never again to be surprised by the evaluation marks I received.

Looking back, I am sure I could have been a better employee for that Engineering Officer. There were things I should have done differently. For starters, since I received no feedback about my work, I should have asked him how he thought I was doing. But sometimes we do not know what we do not know. That is what supervisors are for - so employees do not have to guess how they are doing.

I moved on the best I could, thinking that particular boss was an anomaly - an unusual occurrence. But I know there are other supervisors out there just like him. There are still supervisors who do not tell their employees how they are doing throughout the year and then surprise them with a bad performance evaluation. There are still supervisors who have disagreements with their employees - maybe even get angry at them - and then use performance evaluations like a vindictive hammer. I was fortunate that in both my Coast Guard and law enforcement careers, I never worked for another supervisor like that Engineering Officer.

Here is what I learned from that experience:

- Do not make employees guess. Let them know how they are doing (good or bad).

- Do not be afraid to tell an employee if improvement is needed.

- Do not be afraid to ask for improvement, even if the person is performing at a minimally acceptable level. Better is always better.

- Do not be vindictive and use performance evaluations as a hammer, when coaching or counseling would have been appropriate.

- Do not be THAT guy. Learn from the bad supervisor role models you have encountered or endured.

TIP: Feedback needs to be ongoing and continuous, and not event driven. No one should be surprised by their performance evaluations and those evaluations should never be used as a vindictive hammer.

Tip #42

Unacceptable Behavior Categories

All unacceptable employee behavior will fall into one of three categories: attendance, performance, or conduct. Here are explanations of the three categories:

1. **Attendance.** Attendance refers to the most basic of work expectations. The employee is expected to show up for work on time for every scheduled day or scheduled shift and work that full day or full shift. Obviously, vacation and personal days are an exception. Sick days are also an exception, but with very narrow parameters. No job expects its employees to be at work if they are deathly ill. But neither are employees expected to use every sick day allowed. Tardiness is also an attendance problem. The expectation is that you will be at work on time and ready to start working at the start of the shift. There is no guess work here. You are either on time or you are not.

2. **Performance.** If the employee fails in some aspect of his job, or fails to meet the supervisor's expectations,

but those failures are not a violation of policy, the issue is a performance problem. An employee spending excessive time making personal phone calls at work, failing to have reports finished by the end of the shift, failing to complete simple tasks without being reminded repeatedly, or an employee intentionally causing conflict between coworkers are all examples of performance problems.

3. **Conduct.** A violation of a policy, a code of conduct violation, or a violation of the department rules and regulations would fall under this category. Conduct problems can run the gamut from violating a no-smoking policy, to sleeping on duty, to putting town gas in a personal vehicle. Conduct violations are the easiest to identify and categorize.

Each problem category may require a slightly different response. Some require only casual conversations with the employee to correct a problem. Other categories require considerable planning on the part of the supervisor to address the issue. Listed below are some guidelines that may help you categorize unacceptable behavior:

- All behavioral problems will always fall into one of the three categories. There are no exceptions.

- An employee can have a problem in one category and excel in other areas. Your hardest working employee who is frequently late for work has an attendance problem. Deal with the attendance problem, even if he shines in other areas.

- Categorizing helps supervisors decide the next step, which may be a casual conversation, counseling that amounts to a performance improvement discussion, further formal investigation, or formal discipline.

- Attitude problems frequently fall into the performance category. An employee not helping coworkers, or doing just the bare minimum not to get fired may not rise to the level of a policy violation, but they are performance issues. Deal with the performance issue as a real problem and not just a person with a bad attitude.

- Categories do not merge, but employee behavior can. An employee could have both a performance problem and an attendance problem. Deal with each category separately, and you will find it easier to plan your response to the problem issue.

TIP: When dealing with unacceptable employee behavior, identify the problem and categorize it as a problem related to attendance, performance, or conduct. Take this first step before beginning your planning and response phase.

Tip #43

Recognition – It's in the Details

Research verifies that learning a new musical instrument helps sharpen your cognitive skills. I discovered almost by accident that it is also a great diversion from work. I started playing the fiddle several years ago, and as I mentioned in a previous tip, I take an occasional lesson from Megan Chowning via Skype. I know I will not be performing with Megan at the Grand Ole Opry anytime soon - or ever. But I am having fun learning. I do, however, occasionally question whether I'm at the appropriate ability level for the time I have invested. That is the same question every employee asks himself about his own work performance.

Megan, is not only a professional musician and a great instructor, she is also a savvy businessperson. So it does not surprise me that she emails a monthly newsletter to all her students with lesson information and tips, as well as the profile of a "Student of the Month." These profiles are typically gifted young fiddle students who have won contests, or older veteran fiddlers who have formed a new bluegrass band. I read each of the "award" profiles with a little envy knowing I have no plans to enter a fiddle contest or form a band. I am just having fun playing and practicing.

And then one month it happened. To my surprise, Megan's monthly email came with a headline that said, "**Ron Glidden - Student of the Month!**" Reading the profile, I saw that Megan had found a way to make me feel special. The following is just part of what she wrote:

> *The things that make Ron the Student of the Month are his consistency and commitment. He understands so well the concept of "getting out what you put in" when it comes to learning something new. Ron believes that giving up on learning and growing means giving up on life as a whole. He's not about kicking back and resting on his laurels and that's evident in his fiddling. He is organized in his learning. There are lists and spreadsheets, updated regularly, and even though sometimes there are weeks in-between his lessons, rarely does a week go by when I don't get an update from a festival or workshop he's attended or an email comes with a question about a recording he heard or video he saw. It's clear that discipline and commitment have been a part of Ron's philosophy throughout his life and he's bringing those qualities to learning to play the fiddle and the results speak for themselves.*

Megan's description of me does not say I'm a great fiddler. It does not say I won any contests or started a new band. In fact, it does not mention anything award-worthy. What Megan does point out are a few traits that I identify with and that are important to me: organization, discipline, and commitment. When she talks about lists and spreadsheets, she's talking about behaviors that I engage in regularly. Her pointing these things out made this particular recognition feel individualized for me, rather than the generic "nice job" that so many supervisors use in their recognition efforts.

What gets recognized gets repeated. Too often supervisors wait for the big event before recognizing a subordinate's behavior. Whether it is winning a fiddle contest or saving someone from a burning building, those big events do not occur all that often. So if your employees engage in a behavior that you like and you want them to repeat that behavior, find a way to recognize it. If they display a character trait that you appreciate, let them know. It does not have to be "employee of the month." It can be as simple as writing them an informal note or sending them an email letting them know that you recognize something special in their behavior or character. Be specific, like Megan, about the behavior you recognize. And craft your recognition so it applies to a specific individual. We all like recognition, especially when it comes from a person we trust and respect. And recognition about our behavior gets that behavior repeated.

TIP: Do not wait for the big event. Individualize your recognition efforts. Make recognition for good performance specific, sincere, timely, and frequent.

Tip #44

Getting Along

I once worked for a boss who frequently operated in conflict-avoidance mode. His philosophy was "Let's all get along." His leadership style was interpreted by his supervisors to mean that we should ignore the small problems we observed for the sake of getting along, and that would somehow result in a smooth-running organization. I can tell you from experience, that philosophy did not work. Ignoring unacceptable behavior is never the answer. Ignore unacceptable behavior and you encourage it to be repeated. The trick is to figure out when and where you should become involved.

First and foremost, employees should understand that, as a minimum, they are required to tolerate each other so that all employees can do the job for which they are being paid. If they become friends with each other, consider it a bonus. If they are at least friendly, it makes for a more pleasant work environment. But as a minimum, they must be respectful to each other while at work. Respect in the workplace equates to a safe work environment and that is essential. Sometimes that means cooperatively working with people they may not like.

Supervisors have an even greater obligation. In addition to tolerating people they may not like, they should work to earn the trust of their employees by demonstrating that they care about all of the employees (including those they do not like). Supervisors must do this to help improve overall performance since that is why we have supervisors in the first place.

Know that people will argue and disagree occasionally. Adults, in some cases, need to learn to stand up for themselves - at least to a point. We are not their kindergarten teacher, and they should stop crying to us just because a coworker looked at them cross-eyed or does not want to have lunch with them. While I think many employees could benefit from learning to stick up for themselves instead of making every issue the boss's problem, supervisors should recognize that real conflict in the workplace is unacceptable. If you determine that gossip, bickering, and making derogatory comments about each other is interfering with morale and performance, or is creating a hostile or unsafe work environment, then it is time to step into the fray.

- Plan to have a performance discussion with the offending individuals rather than as a group. The group discussion or blanket email or memo just does not work to correct unacceptable behavior. Plan your discussion in advance. Script it out, if necessary. What are your performance expectations? Stick to specifics not generalities.

- If there are multiple issues, stick to the most important. One individual - one meeting - one issue at a time. Too often, we talk about attitude and teamwork without being specific. Defining the behavior you observe will make it easier to explain.

- Identify your performance expectations and your observation of the current behavior. Get right to the point and articulate the behavior observed. Explain the unacceptable behavior (gossip, backbiting, and derogatory comments) in just a couple sentences. Know in advance what the potential consequences could be for someone ignoring your directions (in case the employee asks).

- When the employee starts pointing fingers at others, let him know the discussion is about his behavior, not the behavior of others. Refocus on your expectations and the fact that he needs to meet those expectations, if he wants to continue to work here.

TIP: You cannot make everyone happy. You cannot make them all be friends. You probably can't even make them always get along with each other. But employees should be required to at least tolerate each other and treat each other with respect to help maintain a productive and safe workplace.

Tip #45

The Purpose of Training

A large department recently changed its disciplinary process in hopes of making it less punitive. Because disciplinary infractions on an employee's record can negatively impact his chance for promotion, the department decided that some disciplinary infractions would disappear from an employee's record, if the employee attended a class. Some of the eligible misbehaviors included tardiness, missing a court date, and being rude to the public. According to the department, the one day class might cover such topics as time management, ethics and emotional health.

While I applaud the effort to find an alternative to traditional progressive discipline, the training option they chose does raise some concerns. Too often, training gets used as a form of punishment - or a last chance intermediate sanction before the "real punishment" is imposed. Sometimes the training is used as documentation to show the department made an effort on the employee's behalf even while assuming that eventual termination is a foregone conclusion. While both discipline and training can be corrective, neither should be punishment.

If an employee engages in misconduct or simply does not perform to his supervisor's expectations, the problem is always either a lack of knowledge or a lack of execution. If the problem is a lack of execution, it may be related to a number of causes including lack of resources (equipment, time, money, or manpower), or a lack of desire. Training will not generally fix a lack of desire.

On the other hand, training is an extremely important aspect of the job. But training should be provided for the right reasons. We train new employees to teach them basic skills for the job. We have in-service training to maintain or improve job proficiency of veteran employees. We have professional development for those who want to develop advanced skills, or additional competencies in a niche in which they are interested, or in a subject area needed by the organization.

Where does remedial training fit into the equation? The answer is simple. If a problem behavior is the result of a lack of knowledge, mandatory training is appropriate to fill the gap. However the training must be related to the knowledge gap. Do not send an employee to a mandatory training that is not specifically related to the problem you are trying to correct, just to document that you sent him to training.

Now, do not get me wrong. I run a training company and I love seminar attendees, whether they come because they want to be there or because they are ordered by their boss to attend. The more the merrier, I always say. And maybe something will rub off that will be useful to that problem employee. But it would be a better use of the employee's time and your training funds to make sure the mandatory training fits the issue of concern. If the issue is leadership, send him to a leadership class. If the officer forgets his duty gun in the bathroom at a restaurant, he will not be cured by making him go to a handgun retention class. The remedy has to fit the problem.

If the behavior was the result of a lack of knowledge, then training or retraining may be the appropriate method of changing the behavior. But could an employee not know he is supposed to show up to work on time? Did he not know there is traffic every day that may require him to leave home earlier? These and similar issues do not require training. They require a supervisor who provides feedback. A brief performance improvement discussion - something more than a casual conversation, but less than a written reprimand or suspension - may address the situation more appropriately than a mandatory training in lieu of punishment option.

TIP: Very few employee problems are the result of a lack of knowledge. Training is an extremely valuable resource when used to fill gaps in knowledge of underperforming employees, or to provide professional development for good employees. But it is not a cure-all in every case.

Tip #46

The Supervisor as Protector

A supervisor recently complained to me about what he perceived was his department's overuse of punishment. He said "They" used the threat of punishment continuously, and that morale was terrible and everyone was walking on eggshells. I knew that the "they" he was talking about were his bosses. I understood the supervisor's concern. He believed that management was overly focused on punishment which, in turn, hurt morale. He saw himself as the protector of his subordinates against management's overzealous use of punishment for minor mistakes.

Being a little protective is one thing, but we, as supervisors, are getting paid to improve the performance of those we supervise. We are also part of the leadership team. There should be no "they" in the equation. That does not mean we always agree with our boss or others on our leadership team. But it does mean we should all be on the same page with regards to our organization's mission.

Caring for your subordinates does not mean picking sides against management, or ignoring unacceptable behavior. Good leadership from above makes the mission easier. But the mission still needs to be accomplished, even where leadership from above is lacking. That is why front-line supervisors are so important. They can help insure the success of the organization's mission, even when someone above them makes repeated mistakes that impacts morale. Good supervisors serve as protectors for their subordinates, not by ignoring mistakes or unacceptable behavior, but by leading by example in spite of bad examples that may surround them.

When a supervisor complains that his boss seems bent on disciplining everyone, I am inclined to ask for specifics. What specific behaviors are being disciplined? One supervisor responded that employees were disciplined if they were late for work. I asked if he thought they should be allowed to be late for work. The supervisor gave me several excuses on why employees could be late for work and, in his opinion, should not be punished.

My next question was: What do you mean by punishment? Some people think they are being punished because a supervisor asked them in a casual conversation not to behave in a certain way. Punishment is the wrong terminology to use, and I believe the wrong course of action. We do not want to punish anyone for being late for work. But if you determine the behavior is unacceptable, should it be ignored entirely? What about causal conversations? What about more formal performance improvement discussions? That is how we can act as protectors for our subordinates.

Intervene early and as often as needed so there is no need for more formal disciplinary measures, let alone punishment. And what if the employee continues to engage in the inappropriate behavior? Then it is the employee who has failed to accept responsibility after clear notice from his caring supervisor. All employees have choices, and there must be consequences for those choosing to not meet your expectations.

The reason supervisors so often fail at holding people accountable is they think their only options are protector where nothing happens, or punishment. This results in supervisors looking at an emerging problem as a fluke or accident that is either not worth addressing or will resolve itself. Some supervisors avoid intervening because they think conflict avoidance will maintain harmony. Some avoid intervening because they see themselves as protectors against management. Neither of these strategies will work to correct unacceptable employee behavior.

Want to be a protector? Engage in early intervention, set clear expectations, and hold subordinates accountable for those expectations so that discipline from above is not even considered.

TIP: Supervisors can best serve as protectors of their employees, even in the face of a difficult management environment, by setting out clear expectations and then intervening early and often to correct behavior or performance issues when those expectations are not met.

Tip #47

Improvement Is Not enough

In January of 2016, the City of Flint Michigan was declared to be in a state of emergency. Water from the corrosive Flint River had caused lead from aging pipes to leach into the water supply, causing extremely elevated levels of lead. As many as 12,000 children may have been exposed to the contaminated drinking water. Original water tests had shown many homes with over 100 parts per billion of lead in their water. I watched a news report in February of 2016 in which a government official said the water quality had improved. When asked if it was now safe to drink, the official said "No." There is no safe level of lead contamination in drinking water. You either have lead contamination or you do not. Improvement sounds nice, but it is not acceptable in this case. Would you allow your children to drink improved, but still lead-contaminated, water from Flint Michigan?

    The improvement dilemma raises its ugly head even when dealing with our employees. We get so frustrated with employees who do not even try to improve - in some cases even after discipline - that we are too willing to accept mere improvement as a sign of success. Like the improved, but contaminated, water in Flint, improved behavior can still leave us with a bad taste, as well as performance and morale issues.

In a previous tip, I talked about the three behavior categories of attendance, performance, and conduct. If a supervisor is courageous enough to confront unacceptable employee behavior in any of these categories, he has at least taken a step that many other supervisors will never even attempt to take. When taking that important first step, if the supervisor hears something akin to "I'll try to improve," it may at first feel like success, but in reality he has accomplished little. When it comes to a person changing their behavior for the better, they either change or they do not. They do not get points for trying.

Imagine a 911 Emergency dispatcher who continuously makes critical errors that puts callers, officers, and the agency at risk. The acceptable level for these errors is zero. The dispatcher has been counseled, retrained, and disciplined repeatedly. Since the errors continue, despite the consequences imposed, the organization responded by assigning two employees to a one-person job. The unacceptable errors continue as the employee tries to improve. Improvement in this case is not success. When lives are on the line, in order to have success, no mistakes are acceptable.

Imagine a supervisor who is counseled for taking all of his 15 allotted sick days for two consecutive years. He becomes angry because he feels entitled to all 15 days. The job expectations are explained (we expect you to be at work for your scheduled shift every day except for very specific situations). Since he is a supervisor, the concept of leading by example is even explained. The following year he takes 13 sick days, and claims he has improved.

Imagine a veteran officer working patrol on the midnight shift who wrote only two traffic citations last year. He has the worst statistics in the department. His supervisor counsels him and then posts the entire shift's statistics to motivate the under-performing officer. Note - competition motivates self-motivated individuals, not necessarily slugs. The supervisor even writes citations himself so he can set an example hoping the employee will become inspired. He is not. The result? The following year the officer writes four traffic citations and jokes about his 100% improvement.

You can probably think of dozens of similar examples where improvement alone is not enough. Think about the employee who is chronically late; the employee with serious hygiene issue; the employee who does not put gas in the cruiser at the end of his shift; the employee who never fills out departmental forms correctly. These are not cases where improvement is needed. They are cases where correction is needed, and that correction must be to the standard set either by the department or the individual supervisor.

Imagine a case involving an employee who blatantly engages in sexual harassment. How about an officer who downloads pornography on the department computer? How about an employee who steals just a little gas from the town gas pump? Would it be OK if these employees improved just a little? It is clear to most that improvement is not enough.

For some situations - particularly conduct situations - there is no improvement option. If you engage in that type of behavior, you no longer have the privilege of working in this organization. While we are usually quick to observe that if an employee steals, improvement is insufficient, we too often settle for an employee saying he will try to improve in other areas. If you repeatedly counsel an employee about being late for work, he does not get a gold star for improvement because he was late a few less times next month.

There are some issues regarding marginal performance where a little improvement would be welcome. If you have an employee doing an average or slightly below average job, a little improvement would be nice. But if you have an employee with an attendance, performance, or conduct issue and that behavior is far below your expectations, improvement is not sufficient. Set a clear standard and hold the employee accountable until he meets that specific expectation.

TIP: Do not settle for employee improvement that falls short of your clearly stated expectations for attendance, behavior, or conduct.

Tip #48

Messy Bessy

As you walk towards the front door of the restaurant, you see trash and cigarette butts on the ground. Inside, the wait staff does not seem overly busy, but there are numerous tables that have not yet been cleaned. You decide to use the restroom. You observe paper towels overflowing onto the floor from the waste basket, and you have a general impression that it has been days since this restroom was cleaned. You make a judgment call at that moment to find another restaurant. Maybe first impressions are not always fair, but they are a fact in the business world.

People who need the services of a public safety organization or their municipality cannot vote with their feet. They stay with us because they need us, but they immediately develop opinions about our professionalism (or lack thereof). Unfortunately, those opinions are not kept private. Studies show that they share their negative impressions about us with at least ten of their friends or family members. A lot of bad impressions could hurt our relationships with an entire community. Sometimes those bad impressions start with something as simple (and fixable) as clutter or a lack of cleanliness of the workplace. Before we get a chance to demonstrate how good we are at our jobs, *Messy Bessy* has caused the public to question the professionalism of the entire Department.

If you have a *Messy Bessy* (or a bunch of them), there are three reasons why you may want to consider holding that employee accountable for such behaviors.

1. **Professional image of the employee.** If their office, their mailbox, or even their patrol vehicle is cluttered, messy, or unorganized, it will negatively impact their professional image. In addition, an organized work space makes it easier to be productive, which also impacts the employee's professional image.

2. **Professional image of the Department.** First impressions are important, happen quickly, and affect the entire Department.

3. **Health.** It is well known that dust, bugs, and other cleanliness issues can cause health problems. We can blame the janitor's failure to clean adequately for our sinus problem, but his duties are usually to empty the trash and vacuum the floor. Instead of waiting for the janitor, wouldn't it be great if employees just picked up their own food wrappers, dishes, or the crumbs they left on the table? Wouldn't it be great if they threw away their old

Styrofoam coffee cups or soda cans? Wouldn't it be nice if they occasionally wiped down the half-inch layer of dust off of their desk, or cleaned out the two-week-old French fries, and the hamburger wrappers out of their police cruiser?

Here are some guidelines to help supervisors deal with *Messy Bessy*:

- If you see a mess created by an employee, ask them to pick it up. Ask them to remove the clutter they created. Ask first; tell, if that does not work; or order, if necessary. You do not need a policy or a new rule. It does not matter if there is a janitor. It does not matter if they think it is not their job. And it does not matter if the other shift does not require it. The expectations you set for your shift and for those you supervise are yours and should be followed.

- Some employees might argue that it is their workplace and they can maintain and clean it or not as they choose. In fact, the workplace belongs to the organization. They can live in a mess at home, if they want to. But do not allow them to work in one.

- If the problem is caused by one individual, deal with that individual. Do not send out memos or emails to those not causing the problem. If there is widespread clutter causing an unprofessional appearance, deal with it on a wider level. Shift supervisors can have their shift clean their work areas - especially the mess or clutter they created.

- It does not matter if the public does not see the part of the station that is messy. A messy work area negatively impacts morale, as well as the public's perceptions.

- It is not always the janitor's job. Employees should pick up their own mess and help keep individual work areas looking clean, organized, and presentable to the public - should they happen to enter the work area by invite or by accident. What is and is not the job is determined in large part by the expectations clearly set by the immediate supervisor. And those expectations should include maintaining a professional workplace appearance.

TIP: Maintaining a clean, uncluttered, and organized workplace that enhances the organization's professional image is the responsibility of all employees and should be an expectation clearly voiced by all supervisors.

Tip #49

Specialty Entitlement

You have probably dealt with marginal performers who, for some reason, felt a sense of entitlement, and either said or implied that the task you assigned them was "Not my job." Most supervisors have no difficulty in holding these employees accountable. You probably weren't that thrilled with their performance to begin with. And the little extra anger you felt because of their resistance probably prompted you to take corrective action. But what if that entitled employee had (maybe with your help) developed an expertise in one aspect of the job? He found a niche he really liked, was really good at, and regularly produces results that you really appreciate. It seemed like a Win-Win situation up until now. He had increased job satisfaction, morale, and motivation. You got good results. But today you need him to be a team player. You ask him to help in an area that is within his job description, but not an area he likes.

Consider the Public Works employee who normally operates heavy equipment. He is good at it, gets paid extra for doing it, and really enjoys the job. He is required to know many aspects of the job, but works mostly on heavy equipment, because that task has been needed almost daily for the past year. Today however, Memorial Day is fast approaching and you as the DPW Director need everyone mowing the grass at the town cemetery. Two employees are out injured, so you ask the hardworking equipment operator to help with the mowing just for today. He argues that it is beneath his expertise. He threatens a grievance, and then threatens to go home sick.

Consider also the patrol officer with an expertise in drug investigations. Over the years, you sent him to the training that helped develop that expertise. You supported his assignment to the drug task force. Now he is back in patrol, but wants to continue to focus only on drug investigations. That is great when such investigations occur, but there are other cases, calls to be handled, and situations where his assistance is needed by his fellow officers. His performance in drug investigations is exemplary. His performance in other areas is substandard.

I am a big fan of helping employees find their niche - that one aspect of their job that they really like. It does not have to come with a title or a pay raise, but it almost always comes with improved job satisfaction, morale, motivation, and performance. With that said, if not carefully managed, it can also come with an entitlement problem. As supervisors, we can get the benefits of an employee working in a niche he really likes, while minimizing the potential entitlement problem, if we help the employee keep the appropriate perspective about his job in relation to the mission of the organization.

Consider the following:

- The Marines have an axiom: "Every Marine a Rifleman." Regardless of their specialty, all Marines are trained to support the primary mission of the organization. We can all learn from that concept. What is the mission of your organization? Everyone's job should support that mission which means sometimes employees have to do parts of the job they do not enjoy.

- If an employee is doing a great job in his niche, periodic recognition from the supervisor will help to encourage that ongoing top performance. Periodic discussions about performance should also include references to other important aspects of the job. No single person's assignment is more important than the organization's overall mission.

- No one is indispensable, including top-performing employees in a specialty assignment or niche. Threats by an employee to quit working in the niche, or quit working as a top performer may be no more than venting. Do not overreact to those emotional comments. If the employee really enjoys the niche, he will continue to be a top performer. If he becomes an under-achiever, know that there are others probably quietly waiting in the wings for their chance at that niche or assignment.

- If you are considering removing someone from their niche or specialty assignment, do not wait for some big event to take action. Your action should be for the good of the organization and not as retaliation.

- Deal with insubordination appropriately. Supervisor-employee disagreements, about which assignment is more important, are acceptable. But at the end of the day the decision is up to the supervisor. If the employee refuses or states he is going home sick as a result of your request, he has made a decision that requires you to make a decision. Insubordination should not be tolerated.

TIP: Working in a niche or specialty assignment improves job satisfaction, morale, motivation, and performance, but can also cultivate a feeling of entitlement. Prevent this entitlement feeling by keeping the employee grounded in the organization's mission and the many roles necessary – not just their one specialty – to accomplish that mission.

Tip #50

When to Speak Up

Without question, finding that proper balance between conflict avoidance and being the micromanaging nitpicker is one of the most common problems supervisors must deal with when developing their own leadership identity. Unfortunately, we too often lean a little towards the conflict-avoidance side. If that sounds like you, you are not alone. It is human nature to try to avoid conflict - especially with your coworkers and subordinates.

In 1951, Solomon Asch conducted an experiment to investigate how group pressure could influence an individual. The test subjects were asked to choose which line from one drawing was the same length as a line on a separate drawing. The test subjects did not realize the other participants had been instructed to give the wrong answer. Most test subjects went along with the group choice even though they knew it was wrong. Asch concluded that people conform to groups for two main reasons: because they want to fit in; or because they believe the group is better informed than they are.

Supervisors are no different. They would like to fit in, and occasionally think that they may be wrong based on what the group thinks. Unfortunately, both reasons can cause supervisors to avoid speaking up and correcting unacceptable employee behavior. If group pressure can influence an individual to the group point of view, even when the individual knows the group is wrong, then peer pressure can influence a supervisor to remain silent.

Sometimes we cannot stop thinking about the unacceptable behaviors we observe in our employees, even if we choose to remain silent. They bother and nag our conscience. As a supervisor, you should be aware of the fact that if an unacceptable behavior really bothers you to the point that you cannot stop thinking about it, you probably will not do a good job hiding your true feelings. Do not rely on sarcasm, dirty looks, grunts, or body language to convey your displeasure. Use your assertive communication skills to provide corrective feedback.

Because it is human nature to want to fit in with our coworkers, we often look for excuses to justify remaining silent, even when someone is engaging in unacceptable behavior and even when the situation bothers our conscience. We may downplay the situation by looking at it as an isolated case.

Consider the employee who is ten minutes late for work. We tell ourselves it is a minor issue - it was only ten minutes. We make up excuses for the employee before he even opens his mouth. We assume there must have been an unexpected traffic delay. Maybe he woke up late. We think the best of our employees and that is good. But we, too frequently, minimize unacceptable behavior. And that is bad. We fail to look at the effect that unaddressed behavior has on his coworkers who arrive at work early every day. We fail to look at the impact it might have on the future behavior of the individual. Is our silence encouraging repeated similar behavior?

Sometimes we spend too much time thinking about the bad results that may happen if we give appropriate corrective feedback for unacceptable behavior. We consider how angry the person might become when we confront him. We imagine our actions will cause his bad attitude to worsen or spread to others. We imagine others might align themselves with the violator, making our job even harder. When this thought process begins, remind yourself that we all try to find justification not to have that difficult conversation.

We do a lot of thinking to justify why we should not speak up. Silence that maintains the status quo is often the easiest road to follow, even when we know it is wrong. It takes courage to speak up about unacceptable behavior, especially if others have followed peer pressure into silence.

TIP: Do not let peer pressure or your thought process justify your silence when a difficult employee discussion is needed. When your conscience is telling you that both the behavior of the employee and your silence is wrong, it is time to speak up.

Tip #51

When There Is No Answer

It was almost thirty years ago when I received a promotion to sergeant in the police department. One of my first subordinates turned out to be one of the most challenging I would ever encounter throughout my entire career. He was intelligent, capable of doing the job, and sometimes an above-average performer. But long before I created the term *Morale Killer,* I would come to think of him as a "Sergeant's Nightmare." He tried to undermine my authority at every opportunity. He gossiped, he complained, he back-stabbed. He was sarcastic and confrontational with an evil sense of humor, which he used to demean coworkers and supervisors alike. He said he loved the profession, but hated the Department because it was run by incompetents. He thought of himself as the hardest working officer. But the only thing he worked hard at was spreading negativity.

    I did not have the experience to deal effectively with the problem. Even a week-long sergeant's leadership course did not give me the answers. My fellow sergeants had no answers either and were just thankful the guy did not work for them. I can recall reading *"Dealing With*

People You Can't Stand" (Brinkman & Kirschner 1994) in hopes of finding an answer. The book discussed different types of problem employees in each chapter with accompanying solutions. But my problem employee seemed to be listed in multiple chapters. He couldn't be easily categorized, which means there seemed to be no single solution. If I was a mental health professional, I might look in my DSM, or *Diagnostic Statistical Manual*. The DSM might list 20 symptoms and then advise me that if my client had five or more of those symptoms then it was likely he had a particular disorder and should be treated accordingly. Too bad the law enforcement profession did not give me such a book so I could have had an absolute answer for this problem employee.

The truth of the matter is that for some problem employees, there is no single answer or solution. In reflecting today on my very first problem employee, I think I could handle him better with what I now know, but I am pretty sure I still wouldn't have an answer that would have fixed the problem. I am not suggesting we give up, but I am suggesting there is not always going to be a single answer that turns every problem employee into a productive member of the organization. My first (and most memorable) problem employee resigned a year after I became his sergeant. Of course, he accused me of picking on him and said that I was his reason for leaving. I'm OK with that. If doing my job and holding him just as accountable as everyone else is why he resigned, then I will take the blame. If you have one of those morale-killing sergeant's nightmare type of employees - the kind for which there seems to be no answer - I offer the following suggestions:

- Hold the person just as accountable as you would anyone else. Do not ignore the problem just because he is confrontational, and do not hold him more accountable just because you do not like him.

- Do not generalize. While it is easy to categorize someone as having a negative attitude, it is much more effective to identify the specific behaviors you want to correct.

- Have a performance improvement discussion. This is more than causal conversation, but less than formal discipline. Clearly set your expectations for everyone, including your most difficult employee.

- Have more performance discussions. In fact, for your problem employee, schedule them on a regular basis. He should understand that one of the consequences of bad behavior is more individual supervision and more performance discussions.

- Respectful treatment of coworkers and supervisors is not an attitude, it is a behavior. Hold people accountable for these behaviors.

- Occasionally, allow a little ranting by the problem employee to you <u>in private</u>. You can acknowledge you understand his feelings or concerns without agreeing with anything.

- Do not forget your good employees. They expect you to fix the problem, and become very frustrated when you do not. Work hard to make deposits in their trust account by having lots of positive contacts with your good workers.

- Do not forget yourself. Problem employees zap your emotional energy. Recharge. Enjoy time with family, enjoy your hobbies, workout or run to de-stress and recharge. Do not let thoughts of that one employee dominate your off-duty time.

- Do not tolerate disrespectful behavior or insubordination.

TIP: Some problem employees are like a bad cold we just can't shake. While there may be no cure for the common cold, a couple of aspirin can minimize the discomfort. A good supervisor can be like that aspirin. Minimize the discomfort to your organization. Hold the problem employee accountable for bad behavior, and spend a lot of extra effort having positive contacts with your good employees.

Tip #52

When Accountability Is a New Concept

When it comes to behavior, the good news is that most employees self-regulate and meet the stated or perceived expectations of their supervisor. The bad news is that too few supervisors clearly articulate those expectations, and so there are employees who fail regularly to meet minimum performance standards. A laissez-faire or conflict-avoidance leadership style does not win us any friends along the way. And good employees find such leadership styles demotivating. Hardworking employees hate the fact that those who are not doing their jobs are seldom held accountable for poor performance or unacceptable behavior. Sadly, sometimes - despite our best intentions - it is easy to ignore a variety of employee behavior and performance problems.

Most supervisors understand the need for accountability. But understanding it and actually doing it are two different concepts. Even if you understand the importance of accountability, sometimes the day-to-day challenges of the job can cause a supervisor to slip into conflict-avoidance mode.

So let's assume that one morning you wake up and realize you have let things go too far. You decide you need to make a change. You decide you are no longer going to let a particular issue slide and that you will no longer tolerate poor performance. How did you come to this realization? Maybe an incident occurred that was the straw that broke the camel's back, or maybe the fact that you have been letting things slide has started to bother you even when you are home and should be relaxing. If your conscience is bothering you - pay attention.

So how do you break out the new you? How do you make the change from conflict avoidance to holding people accountable without seeming like you turned into the evil dictator overnight? Here are some steps that might help in your transition:

- **One Step at a Time.** Pick out the one or two issues that need the most immediate attention and focus on them first. Figure out what issues bother you the most and deal with those first. Keep the laundry list of bad behaviors for your own reference. No need to address every issue at once. Your current situation did not happen in one day and is not going to be fixed in one day.

- **Face-to-Face.** Please do not send an email or memo to everyone announcing the big change in your accountability efforts. Have group or individual meetings. Group meetings may be appropriate for group issues, especially to inform subordinates about your expectations, which may not have been previously articulated.

- **One-on-One.** If you have a problem employee or someone not meeting your expectations, meet with that individual. Do not punish the whole group. Do not make everyone read a memo that applies only to one employee.

- **Identify the problem.** Identify the problem, and articulate a clear expectation for future performance or behavior.

- **It is about the future.** Group or individual meetings at this stage are not about lecturing, yelling, or punishing people for past behaviors. The meetings are about setting expectations for the future.

- **Acknowledge change.** If the problem is longstanding and has been long ignored by you, acknowledge that you have known about it, and for a variety of reasons have failed to hold people accountable to a clear expectation. If they did not know about or understand the expectation, the fault is yours. Once you clearly state the expectation, any future failure is theirs.

- **Why change?** A problem employee may ask why you are making the change. He may imply that rank has gone to your head. Maybe he will let you know that you are a nice guy so you must be getting ordered to make this change. It is acceptable to explain that you are making the change because you recognized that certain minimum standards (or your own expectations) are not being met. And it is your job, as a supervisor, to help all of your employees achieve that standard or meet those expectations.

- **But we've always done it this way.** The fact that unacceptable behavior or marginal performance has seemingly been ignored does not make such behavior or performance right. You may have made some bad decisions or ignored certain unacceptable behaviors that allowed the cultural norm to shift. That does not mean you can never improve as a leader or never improve the performance of your employees. You do not have to be stuck in the past.

TIP: It is never too late to set out clear expectations for our employees, and never too late to begin holding them accountable to those expectations.

Speaker Information and Book Orders

If you would like additional information about scheduling the author as a trainer or speaker for your next conference or training program, or if you would like to order additional copies of this book, please contact:

Ronald C. Glidden
Glidden Training & Consulting, LLC
P.O. Box 73
South Wellfleet, MA 02663

Tel: 508-349-2839
Email: chief@ronglidden.com
Website: www.ronglidden.com

Ron's Other Books

52 Bulletproof Leadership Tips
Stopping the School Shooter
Massachusetts Law Enforcement Guide to Firearms Laws